HIKING IS FUNDAMENTAL

A Step-by-Step Guide to Hitting the Trail

BARBARA ANN KIPFER

FALCON®

ESSEX, CONNECTICUT

FALCON®

An imprint of Globe Pequot, the trade division of
The Rowman & Littlefield Publishing Group, Inc.
4501 Forbes Blvd., Ste. 200
Lanham, MD 20706
www.rowman.com

Falcon and FalconGuides are registered trademarks and Make Adventure
Your Story is a trademark of The Rowman & Littlefield Publishing Group, Inc.

Distributed by NATIONAL BOOK NETWORK

British Library Cataloguing in Publication Information available

Library of Congress Cataloging-in-Publication Data available
Names: Kipfer, Barbara Ann, author.
Title: Hiking is fundamental : a step-by-step guide to hitting the trail /
  Barbara Ann Kipfer.
Description: Guilford, Connecticut : Falcon, [2022] | Includes
  bibliographical references. | Summary: "Author Barbara Ann Kipfer covers
  all the basic elements of getting into hiking, from preparation to pacing,
  in illustrated list-style chapters"— Provided by publisher.
Identifiers: LCCN 2022006379 (print) | LCCN 2022006380 (ebook) | ISBN
  9781493063628 (Paperback : acid-free paper) | ISBN 9781493063635 (ePub)
Subjects: LCSH: Hiking. | Backpacking.
Classification: LCC GV199.5 .K57 2022 (print) | LCC GV199.5 (ebook) | DDC
  796.51—dc23/eng/20220406
LC record available at https://lccn.loc.gov/2022006379
LC ebook record available at https://lccn.loc.gov/2022006380

♾️™ The paper used in this publication meets the minimum requirements of
American National Standard for Information Sciences—Permanence of Paper
for Printed Library Materials, ANSI/NISO Z39.48-1992.

WHEN YOU SEE SOMEONE PUTTING
ON HIS BIG BOOTS, YOU CAN BE
PRETTY SURE THAT AN ADVENTURE
IS GOING TO HAPPEN.

—A. A. MILNE

CONTENTS

INTRODUCTION TO HIKING

TYPES OF HIKES

PREPARATION AND PLANNING

SKILLS AND FITNESS

NAVIGATION

SAFETY AND HEALTH

WEATHER AND WILDLIFE

INTRODUCTION TO HIKING

TODAY IS YOUR DAY!
YOUR MOUNTAIN IS WAITING.
SO . . . GET ON YOUR WAY!

—DR. SEUSS

THERE IS SOMETHING ABOUT THE IDEA OF HIKING—it appeals to most of us. There is a romantic visual that pops into our mind when we hear or read about it. From a 1-hour urban hike to a months-long 1,000-plus-mile thru-hike, there is variety—in length, difficulty, weather, terrain, wildlife, scenery, and challenges. Very few other outdoor activities boast that rich a recreational buffet.

Hiking Is Fundamental is a list book offering all the basic information pertaining to those factors. It is for everyone, from kids to those like me, 65-year-olds hiking for the first time. Because of the variety of options, it is easy to make hiking part of your life. And because it is built on the simple act of walking, most hiking requires simple preparation. You can set personal challenges and goals, and work through hikes of different lengths, of escalating difficulty, in various types of weather, over interesting terrain and scenery, and through the seasons.

For those focused on gear, backpacking, camping, or thru-hiking long trails, there is more to read and digest from other sources. But for those of you who relish the idea of clambering through natural settings, this book will set you up nicely for safe and happy hiking.

BENEFITS OF HIKING

- One of the best and least expensive ways to get exercise.

- Builds stronger muscles and bones.

- Improves your sense of balance.

- Improves cardiorespiratory fitness of heart, lungs, and blood vessels and decreases the risk of certain respiratory problems.

- Reduces chances for heart problems. Lowers blood pressure.

- Improves blood sugar regulation.

- Helps many people lose weight and maintain weight loss as opposed to weight loss through dieting.

- Stabilizes cholesterol levels.

    - Helps reduce negative effects of arthritis by lessening stress on joints and easing joint pain, stiffness, and swelling.

    - Helps reverse the negative effects of osteoporosis by increasing bone density.

- Slows the rate of calcium loss, thus strengthening bones.

- Boosts mood and improves mental health. Hiking soothes and clears the mind.

- Reduces stress, calms anxiety, and lowers risk of depression. Hiking rejuvenates you and increases your happiness.

- Opens up your senses to your surroundings and improves sensory perception. When you open yourself to receive what nature has to offer, you will find many nuggets of wisdom available.

- Hiking makes you more mindful.

- Promotes relational health through hiking with a friend, neighbor, or family member.

- Improves your sleep.

HIKING GOALS

- Fitness, especially outdoor exercise.
- Improve cardiovascular health and strength.
- Try something new. Challenge yourself.
- Fun.
- Exercise with a partner or friend for camaraderie and relationship-building.

- Get fresh air.
- Go somewhere without vehicles.
- Go somewhere without computers, phones, or TVs.
- Cool off or warm up.
- Enjoy a scenic view and/or be near a body of water.
- See seasonal changes, like fall leaves.
- Be outside when there are fewer bugs (spring and fall).
- Be outside when there are no bugs (winter).
- Bird watching, wildlife watching, studying geology, seeing wildflowers and plants.
- Outdoor photography or journaling.
- Incrementally work up to backpacking and camping.
- Cheap therapy.

FUN FACT

The American Discovery Trail is the longest hiking trail in North America, a series of linked roads and recreational trails coast-to-coast across the middle of the United States.

HIKING FOR BEGINNERS

- You have picked the perfect activity for enjoying the beauty of nature at whatever pace and level you are comfortable with.

- Hiking requires just a little planning and preparation: finding a hiking partner, choosing a hike, and gearing up.

- If you have a friend or friends who hike, ask them to take you out for your first time.

- If you don't know any experienced hikers but your partner is willing to learn with you, try taking this up together.

- If you don't have those options, many cities and towns have hiking clubs with regular outings, which you can search for online.

- If going alone is your only (or chosen) option, then start with short trips to popular hiking destinations, and always make sure someone knows where you are going and how long you plan to be gone.

- Choose a hiking route through internet research, local public land management agencies, or guidebooks. If you have friends who hike, ask them for suggestions or contact the parks and recreation department in your town.

- Choose a hiking route by looking at these factors: how much time you have, your fitness level, distance, elevation gain, time of year and weather, and logistics (for hikes that require more planning).

IN EVERY WALK WITH NATURE, ONE RECEIVES FAR MORE THAN HE SEEKS.
—JOHN MUIR

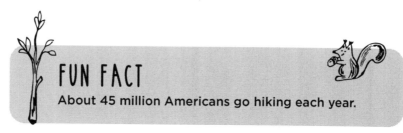

FUN FACT

About 45 million Americans go hiking each year.

- You don't need a lot of gear, just a few essential items—starting with the Ten Essentials: items for navigation, sun protection, insulation, illumination, first aid, fire, repairs, nutrition, hydration, and emergency shelter.

- Footwear is one of the most important items you need to choose. The choices range from supportive ankle-high boots to lightweight trail-running shoes. Comfort is important, but safety, protection, and terrain-appropriateness are, too. Whatever you choose needs to be well broken-in and worn with wool or synthetic socks.

- Choose clothing made of quick-drying, moisture-wicking fabrics such as polyester or wool. Cotton takes a long time to dry when wet, which is why it is not ideal.

- Layer your clothes: next-to-skin base layers, hiking layers, insulation, and rainwear.

- For short treks, a daypack of 15 to 20 liters is enough for the Ten Essentials, water, snacks, and a clothing layer.

- For longer treks requiring more gear, clothing, water, and food, use a 30-liter backpack.

- In general, pack 200 to 300 calories of food and a half liter of water for each hour of hiking. Then factor in hike intensity, weather, your age, body type, and sweat rate. A little extra food and water is always wise.

- If you will need more than 3 liters of water, you may prefer to filter or treat water from a stream or lake to refill your bottle or hydration reservoir. Taking a water treatment system lightens your weight load.

- Additionally, learn about basic first aid, going to the bathroom in the woods, and trail etiquette.

TEN ESSENTIALS

- These should be with you during backpacking and camping trips, and even on day hikes. It is a good habit.

- A few items may sit unused in your backpack forever, but when something goes wrong, you will appreciate having most of these.

- The exact items from each of the ten "systems" can be tailored to the trip you are taking. On a day hike, you might take a map, compass, and GPS but leave the personal locator beacon and altimeter at home. Consider the weather, difficulty, duration, and distance of your trip.

- Refer to the day hiking checklist, first-aid checklist, and backpacking checklist in this book for figuring out what else to bring with you.

- The original Ten Essentials list was created in the 1930s by the Mountaineers, a Seattle organization for outdoor adventurers and climbers. That list included a map, compass, sunglasses and sunscreen, extra clothing, headlamp/flashlight, first-aid supplies, firestarter, matches, knife, and extra food. (They should have added water!)

AMERICANS VIEWED HIKING AS AN OPPORTUNITY TO ESCAPE REGIMENTATION, SLOW DOWN, ENJOY THE SCENERY, RESTORE ENERGY, TEST ONE'S WILL, AND EVEN WORSHIP GOD. TRADITIONALLY, A JOURNEY ALONG THE TRAIL WAS SEEN AS AN END IN ITSELF, WITHOUT A NEED TO COMPLETE THE ENTIRE TRAIL OR EARN RECOGNITION.
—SILAS CHAMBERLIN

- Get your hiking backpack and start filling it with the Ten Essentials.

  1. **NAVIGATION:** some combination of map, compass, GPS device, altimeter watch, personal locator beacon (PLB) or satellite messenger

  2. **HEADLAMP** with batteries (and extra batteries) or rechargeable

  3. **SUN PROTECTION:** sunglasses, sunscreen, and/or sun-protection clothing

  4. **FIRST AID:** either a pre-assembled kit or one built on your own. Any kit should include blister treatment, various adhesive bandages, gauze pads, adhesive tape, disinfecting ointment, pain medication, pen and paper, and nitrile gloves.

  5. **KNIFE:** from single foldout blade to Swiss Army knife and/or multi-tool. Your knife should be able to slice through a piece of paper; otherwise it needs sharpening.

  6. **FIRE SUPPLIES** for starting and maintaining a fire, such as a disposable lighter, waterproof matches in a container, and firestarter like dry tinder in a plastic bag.

  7. **EMERGENCY SHELTER:** bivy sack, ultralight tarp, emergency space blanket, or large plastic trash bag

  8. **FOOD** and extra food: an extra day's worth that has a long shelf life and does not require cooking

  9. **WATER** and extra water, or possibly a filter/purifier or chemical treatment

  10. **EXTRA CLOTHES** for a change in conditions or what you would need to survive a long, inactive period in the elements

- To this you might want to add a **GEAR REPAIR KIT** with things like duct tape, cordage, fabric repair tape, scissors, bungee cords, zip ties, safety pins, sewing kit, parts for a water filter, mattress repair kit, stove repair kit, extra batteries, cash or coins.

HIKING ETIQUETTE

- Know your right-of-way. On the trail you are hiking, follow the right of way yields or the standard right-of-way. If hiking in a group, do not take up the width of the trail; allow others a way to pass.

- Standard right-of-way: Hikers coming uphill have the right-of-way, so if you are descending, step aside.

- Hikers yield to horses and other pack animals. Bicyclists yield to hikers, horses, and other pack animals.

- Some situations require common sense. For example, if a biker is struggling up a steep trail, it's easier for a hiker going down to yield the right-of-way.

- When bringing a pet on a hike, be sure to keep it on a leash and under control.

- Make yourself known when you encounter others, saying "hello" or nodding to them as a friendly gesture.

- When you approach another hiker from behind, announce yourself in a friendly, calm voice and let them know you want to pass.

- Stay on the trail; do not step off it unless you are yielding or taking a break. Do whatever you can to protect plant and animal species, as well as the ecosystem itself.

- Leave rocks, vegetation, and artifacts alone so that others can enjoy them.

- Don't destroy existing rock cairns, and refrain from adding to a rock pile to make it higher.

- If the trail is muddy or very wet, walk through the mud or puddle instead of around it, unless you can do so without going off the trail. Widening a trail by going around puddles and mud is bad for trail sustainability.

GIVE ME THE CLEAR BLUE SKY OVER MY HEAD, AND THE GREEN TURF BENEATH MY FEET.
—WILLIAM HAZLITT

- Leave No Trace principles ask that you move 200 feet (about 70 steps) from a trail, campsite, or body of water before digging a hole to deposit human waste.

- Another Leave No Trace principle is to hold onto your trash. If you packed it in, pack it back out. If you hike with a pet, pack out pet waste as well.

- Do not disturb wildlife, and keep your distance from wildlife you encounter. There may be regulations in certain areas about this.

- Do not feed the wildlife.

- Listen to nature instead of talking or using electronic devices during the hike. You are being respectful of both nature, which relies on natural sounds for communication purposes, and other hikers on the trail.

- Use your smartphone for taking photos, but not for instantaneously sharing with the outside world. Save that for later.

- Be aware of your surroundings at all times, which helps keep you, wildlife, and their habitats safe and healthy.

FUN FACT

By the 1960s and 1970s, the growing popularity of hiking and the expanding network of trails throughout the nation meant that most hikers would rarely spend time building or maintaining the paths on which they traveled.

LEAVE NO TRACE PRINCIPLES

These apply to overnight backpackers and campers as well as day visitors such as day hikers, dog walkers, picnickers, cyclists, and runners, as well as car campers.

Plan Ahead and Prepare:

- Know the regulations and special concerns for the area you plan to visit. Prepare for extreme weather, hazards, and emergencies. Schedule your trip to avoid times of high use.

- Planning includes hiking in small groups or splitting larger groups into smaller groups. Repackage food to minimize waste. Use a map and compass to eliminate the use of marking paint, rock cairns, or flagging.

Travel and Camp on Durable Surfaces:

- In popular areas, concentrate use on existing trails and campsites. Camp at least 200 feet from lakes and streams. Keep campsites small and focus activity in areas where vegetation is absent. Walk single file in the middle of the trail, even when it is wet or muddy.

- In pristine areas, disperse use to prevent the creation of new campsites or trails. Avoid places where impacts are just beginning.

Dispose of Waste Properly:

- For everything from litter to human waste to rinse water, pack it in and pack it out. Leave a place cleaner than you found it. Carry water 200 feet away from streams or lakes, and use small amounts of biodegradable soap to wash yourself or dishes. Scatter drained dishwater.

- Deposit solid human waste in cat holes dug 6 to 8 inches deep, at least 200 feet from water, campsites, and trails. Cover and disguise the cat hole when finished. Pack out toilet paper and hygiene products. Some areas require that human waste be packed out, too.

Minimize Campfire Impacts:

- Make fires only where they are permitted and use established fire rings, fire pans, or mound fires. Keep fires small, and use only sticks from the ground that can be broken by hand.

- Burn all wood and coals to ash. Put out campfires completely and scatter the cooled ashes. Do not bring firewood from home. Buy it from a local source or gather it if and where it is allowed.

Leave What You Find:

- Take only pictures and leave only footprints. You can look at, but not touch, cultural or historical structures and artifacts. Leave rocks, plants, and nature in general as you find them.

- Avoid introducing or transporting non-native species. Clean shoe and boot soles, bike tires, and boat hulls between trips. Do not build structures or furniture or dig trenches.

Respect Wildlife:

- Do not approach animals. Observe from a distance and do not follow or feed them. Avoid wildlife during sensitive times, such as mating, nesting, raising young, or in winter.

- Protect wildlife—and your food—by storing your rations and trash securely. If you bring pets (where allowed), leash and control them at all times.

Be Considerate of Others:

- Respect other visitors and treat them as you would like to be treated. Be courteous.

- Yield to other users on the trail. Step to the downhill side of the trail when encountering horses or other pack animals.

- Take your breaks and camp away from the trails and other visitors. Manage any pet you bring.

- Let the sounds of nature prevail. Avoid using loud voices, making loud noises, or talking a lot.

HIKING SMART

Take the time to ask yourself some important questions before going on a hike, starting with evaluating your experience level. You need to know your limits.

- What is the terrain and change of elevation? What is the length of the hike and the difficulty?

- Ask yourself if you are physically fit for the hike you want to do.

- Evaluate whether you have hiked in the type of environment before, such as temperature and humidity.

- Evaluate your ability to do a higher-elevation hike if that is what you were considering. There is reduced oxygen in the air at higher elevations. If you plan to hike in higher altitudes than you are used to, take extra time to do the hike. Get a good night's sleep and drink a lot of water.

- Are you hiking alone, or do you plan to hike with someone? If you prefer or have to go solo, take extra measures to be prepared for what you might encounter.

- Your safety is your responsibility, so you need to pick the right trail for you and whomever goes with you. Do your research.

- Create a trip plan with the details of where you will be hiking, your contact information, who is going with you, and when you plan to return. Leave this with a friend, family member, or even a neighbor.

FUN FACT

According to the *Journal of Experimental Biology*, hiking on uneven terrain increases the amount of energy your body uses by 28 percent compared to walking on flat ground.

HIKING FOR ITS OWN SAKE, FOR THE SHEER ANIMAL PLEASURE OF GOOD CONDITION AND BRISK EXERCISE, IS NOT AN EASY THING FOR [THE WESTERNER] TO COMPREHEND.
—STATE OF UTAH, 1941

Develop an emergency plan for what to do if you or your hiking companion(s) become lost or injured.

- Learn CPR and basic first aid.

- Make sure you have a way to communicate beyond a cell phone, as you will not be ensured of cellular coverage and reception. Carry a backup battery to charge it, and consider having a personal locator beacon—especially for anything beyond a short day hike.

- Check the weather during planning and right before you head out. Be prepared to seek shelter if necessary, and have rain equipment.

- Check on trail closures, park alerts, wildfire risks, tides, and other potential hazards before you go, especially on a long hike.

- Have a Plan B ready. If you start on a trail and it does not look like something you want to tackle, reverse course and do a different trail or some other activity.

- Always pack the Ten Essentials. Consider the weather when packing food and water, as well as additional equipment such as bug spray.

- Let the slowest hiker set the pace. Stay together and take breaks often. And remember that if you can talk while you are walking, you are traveling at a reasonable speed.

- Hiking takes energy. Be sure to drink when you are thirsty and keep your energy level high with snacks like nutrition/energy bars, nuts, or trail mix.

DOCUMENTING YOUR HIKE

- You can capture the landscape, trail life, your hiking partners, trail milestones (and failures), and learning experiences in a hiking journal.

- You can keep track of your hikes on a daily, weekly, or monthly basis in a computer file or specially set-up online calendar.

- Sketch, draw, and/or paint your adventures.

- Photograph yourself at the beginning and end of a hike, maybe with a photo of your fitness watch displaying the time and length of the hike.

- Photograph nature you enjoy during the hike.

- Record a scene or view, like a waterfall, by taking a video.

- Start your own hiking blog or vlog.

- Record your hike on your phone using maps or apps.

- Think before you geotag—if you're in an area sensitive to overuse, consider keeping the location off social media. Share photos with just your hiking buddies.

- Post a photo or photos of your adventures on any social media you use.

- Pocket a trail map from the trailhead.

- Print out a map to take with you (one of the Ten Essentials) and then keep it in a folder or as part of your journal.

- Keep a list of trails you want to hike.

- Review the trail on your favorite app or online hiking resource.

- If you discover a new trail that is not on the app you use, share it with that hiking community.

- Before you go to bed, write down three things you appreciated from your hike.

LIFE LESSONS FROM HIKING

- How to be prepared, which is clearly good for you but also good for others involved.

- How to problem-solve.

- How to find beauty in the smallest things, with nature being the teacher.

- How to trust yourself, but know that arrogance will come back to haunt you.

- How to power through; you can't just give up in the middle.

- How to recognize the voice in your head that says "can't," accept that it will be there, and carry on.

- How to let go of things that weigh you down and know when to let go of them. You are stuck with your own baggage, but it is up to you how heavy it is.

- How to explore. Meaningful experiences require discipline and are not easy.

- How to find internal harmony. It's all about attitude. A positive attitude will see you through.

- How to connect with another human. You are only as strong as your weakest link.

- How to slow down and savor the moment.

- The struggle is worth it. Be persistent in the pursuit of your goals.

- How not to fuel fear. Recognize that the tough times do not last.

- How to stay in the moment. Every minute spent suffering will build character.

- Getting out of your comfort zone helps you grow and perceive challenges and opportunities in a different way.

- How to just keep moving, one step at a time.

- Though the view at the end is beautiful, the entire journey should be enjoyed.

NEVER TOO LATE TO START

- It's walking, really. Hike smart, evaluate what you can handle, and build on that. Start slowly.

- You can go with an experienced hiker so you feel supported and don't have to worry about navigation or logistics.

- Don't push yourself too hard too soon. Go out for a half hour, then an hour, and eventually 2 hours.

- You may think you are too old to start hiking. Hiking clubs around the world are full of people in their 50s and 60s, even older.

- You may think you are not fit enough, but you are. You walk every day. The secret is to start slowly. If you want, check with your doctor before striking out on the trail for the first time.

- You do not need fancy gear. You may never need more than basic hiking shoes, a hat, sunscreen, and a cheap daypack. Figure out what kind of hiking you enjoy before making significant investments. But do consider trekking/hiking poles, which can lighten your steps, ease stress on your knees, help propel you forward, aid in detecting a path's surface, prevent you from falling, and give you confidence.

- When you set a hiking goal, it should feel challenging and maybe a little bit scary, but it should not make you feel panicked. Maybe shoot for one hike per week the first month.

- Look at the difficulty rating, the length, the elevation change, and the estimated time to complete the hike you are considering.

- Slowly increase variables like time and distance. The more hiking you do, the stronger you will get.

- Do more general walking and stair climbing on your non-hiking days, and get involved in other forms of exercise that elevate your heart rate several times a week.

- Start out at your normal walking pace. If it feels easy, gradually increase your speed to a point where you are breathing slightly heavier but are not overexerting. It is best to learn your pace and stick to it.

- Hiking does not have to involve camping or backpacking. Day hikes are those completed within a day, and that may be what you choose to stick with.

- You might worry about getting lost, but there are an enormous number of very well-marked hiking trails all over the world and likely right by you. Hiking apps and websites for parks and trails contain route descriptions and hiker reviews that indicate how well the trail is signposted. Choose a well-defined hike or join a local hiking club to increase your navigation knowledge and confidence.

- Hiking is a simple activity and it is best to keep it that way. Get basic gear and gradually take longer walks on increasingly demanding trails. Choose age-appropriate challenges. It does not take extremes to be conditioned and healthy.

- The key to happiness may lie in nature—and by venturing into the great outdoors, you gain a vigor that makes life fun and joyful.

- There is something truly magical about being outdoors and exploring our beautiful planet on foot. It is calming, reinvigorating, and relaxing and one of the few activities that switches off your "monkey mind."

- Hiking can be done by just about anyone for as long as they like. Stick with it and you will begin to crave it. Relish the journey.

FUN FACT
The world looks different at 2 miles an hour.

TYPES OF HIKES

THE ANCIENT, SIMPLE ACT OF TAKING A HIKE
IS A WONDERFUL WAY TO READJUST ONE'S
GAZE IN THE WORLD AWAY FROM ONE'S NAVEL,
AND INSTEAD TO LOOK OUTWARD, BEYOND
THE MICROSCOPIC UNIVERSE OF THE SELF.
—MICHAEL W. ROBBINS

THERE ARE MANY TYPES OF HIKES—BASICALLY A smorgasbord to choose from. There's day hiking, solo hiking, hiking with dogs and cats, seasonal hiking, hiking in groups or clubs, family hiking, and urban hiking. There's forest hiking and field hiking. Then there's the next level—overnight hikes or weekenders, backpacking, thru-hiking on long-distance trails, hiking as pilgrimage, mountain hiking, desert hiking, glacier hiking, geocaching, night hiking, hiking in the rain and snow, and much more.

There are also many types of hikers. You can ponder what type of hiker you are and why you want to hit the trail. Do you hike to explore and learn? Hike for relaxation? Hike as pure exercise?

There's one more type of hiking: mental hiking, or daydreaming about your next hike. You can take a break from your job, sit in the sun, and plot your next adventure.

FUN FACT

Earl Shaffer in 1947 became the first to traverse the Appalachian Trail in one continuous journey (2,050 miles). Benton MacKaye, who published his proposal for the trail in 1921, however, had never intended for hikers to travel the entire trail. And Emma "Grandma" Gatewood, mother of eleven children, was the first woman to thru-hike the AT, in 1955 at the age of 67.

SOLO HIKING

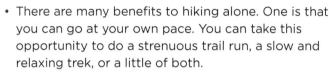

- There are many benefits to hiking alone. One is that you can go at your own pace. You can take this opportunity to do a strenuous trail run, a slow and relaxing trek, or a little of both.

- Silence is hard to come by in regular life or on hikes with others. Find respite in the quiet. Make a few stops along the trail to just sit and relish the quietness of nature.

- Speaking of silence, don't wear headphones. You need total awareness of what is around you—animals, hikers, a change in weather. Listen to the sounds of nature when you are in nature.

- Hiking alone, you can change routes if necessary. If you do not like the trail you are on, choose another when you come to a junction. Do this only if you are familiar with the area, though.

- Don't think too much about the fact that you are alone. Without someone there, you might feel lonely or less motivated. You can distract yourself from those feelings by taking some photos or stopping to name the birds and trees you see.

- If you are on a popular trail, you will likely pass some fellow hikers. Be cordial to everyone and strike up a conversation if you feel comfortable doing so. Use your street smarts to avoid unwanted encounters with those you do not want to communicate with.

- For your first solo trek, hike an easy route or one you have hiked before. This allows you to stay confident from beginning to end.

- Carry a trail map, watch for trail markers, and even take pictures of any trail junctions to help you remember the way you came from.

- You have to rely on yourself to stay safe, so know your limits. Take a break if you are fatigued. If there is a tough water crossing, consider alternatives or wait for another hiker to come along and spot you.

- Be ready for any weather. You can check it up to the moment you depart, but it still can change. Make sure you have rain gear and a jacket, gloves, and hat.

- Pack enough food and water to stay energized and hydrated. It is smart to bring more water than you think you will need.

- Make a trip plan of when you plan to leave, where you will be going (the address of the trailhead and exact location of the trail), any camp you will stay at (if an overnighter), and when you plan to return. Give the trip plan to one or two people and check in with them when you return.

- Be aware at all times. Without another pair of eyes and ears, it is critical to be aware of your surroundings. If something does not feel right, then it's probably not. Solo hiking is not the time to take risks. Trust your judgment, always.

- Be aware of the terrain. Look up to protect your eyes from stray branches. Look down to protect your ankles from uneven roots.

- Research the region and know what animals to expect along the trail. Be ready with bear spray or defensive measures. Educate yourself about how to stay safe in the outdoors.

- From a solo hike, you will find a new mental stamina and self-confidence you may not have had before. You will learn to trust yourself more.

- Cherish the freedom of not having to worry about anyone else or move at someone else's pace.

A HIKE IS AN ADVENTURE SIMPLY BECAUSE YOU CANNOT KNOW IN ADVANCE ALL THAT YOU WILL SEE AND HEAR, WHOM YOU MIGHT MEET, AND WHAT MIGHT HAPPEN.
—MICHAEL W. ROBBINS

HIKING WITH PARTNER(S)

- Even if you are not afraid to hike alone, you might find it more fun with a good partner or partners.

- Partners are helpful if one of you is having a tough day. You can laugh together at the adversity of weather or terrain. You can help each other out if there is an injury or a needed repair.

- On the other hand, a "bad" hiking partner who complains or does not have the same hiking style or has a different goal can suck the fun out of a trip.

- Take the initiative and invite your partner, friend, or acquaintance to hike with you. If you are just starting out as a hiker, maybe you know a more experienced hiker who would walk with you.

- Know yourself before you go looking for a hiking partner. You probably have a good idea of your pace. Pick a partner whose pace is not wildly different from yours; then neither of you will get frustrated.

- Ask yourself what you want to get out of the hike. Is it a physical challenge? Exercise in fresh air and nature? Or looking to accomplish something else? Try to mesh what you want with your hiking partner's goals.

- Discuss the hike with your partner. Look at the map together, as well as the directions for getting there. Do you each have some first-aid training?

- Discuss whether you will chat or hike in relative quiet. Will you share any gear or other supplies, like food and water?

- Discuss what your partner's experience with hiking is, what time of day they like to exercise in general, and whether they have navigation skills. Do they know how to use a map and compass? GPS or trail app?

- What is your current fitness level, and is it comparable to your partner's? Do you or they have any past injuries that may flare up on a hike?

FUN FACT

In 2018, hiking was most popular with 30- to 49-year-olds, followed by the 18 to 29 and 50 to 64 age groups.

- Do either of you have allergies or require prescription drugs that may need to be addressed while hiking?

- Each of you should carry a map and enough water and snacks to sustain you if you get injured or lost. How much can each of you carry on your back?

- If one of you gets injured, can you each figure out how to help the other and get help? If you get lost, can you work together to figure out how to get back on track?

- An alternative to one partner is hiking with multiple partners, like a couple of neighbors, a spouse and child, or a local group.

- Make sure you each take responsibility for preparing before you head out, including proper clothes, bug spray, sunscreen, food, and water.

- Bring along patience and understanding. Everyone is different, including their tolerance levels for pain, endurance, and adversity. Your partner may not walk at the same pace as you, have to rest more frequently, or have less fortitude on a difficult section of the trail. Encouragement will assist you in successfully hiking a trail together.

- Sharing a trail with someone is an intimate experience and time slows down. You can improve a relationship and get closer.

CHILDREN AS COMPANIONS

- Start a family tradition of going hiking one or more times a month. Children love adventure and doing new things. There is a wide range of trails, terrain, and sights out there. It is the perfect way to get them outside.

- If you are taking a child on a hike, the most important thing is to have fun and stay flexible. For kids, it is truly about the journey, not the destination.

- Pick a short, interesting hike and allow extra time. Involve children in planning and preparation if they are old enough.

- Keep kids dry, warm, fed, and hydrated. In warm weather, keep them cool. Everything goes better when basic needs are met.

  - Dress yourself and children in layers.

  - Bring snacks and plenty of fluids. Triple-check the gear list (including the Ten Essentials). Until a child is old enough to be self-sufficient, the responsibility falls solely to the adult.

- Hiking with infants means a child carrier, sun coverings, special foods like formula, and diapers. And be aware of an infant's sleep cycles.

- For ages 1 to 4, you are in the half-carry/half-hike time. They can walk, but not far. A small pack, colorful kid water bottle, carrier, and maybe a toy helps make hiking fun.

FUN FACT

The transition from walking out of necessity to walking out of desire constituted one of the primary—but not sole—origins of American hiking as a leisure activity.

> # BECAUSE IN THE END, YOU WON'T REMEMBER THE TIME YOU SPENT WORKING IN THE OFFICE OR MOWING YOUR LAWN. CLIMB THAT GODDAMN MOUNTAIN.
> ## —JACK KEROUAC

- Safety comes first. Make sure the child has a whistle. Review before each hike what to do if the child becomes separated from you. Teach them to stay put and blow their whistle in three sharp bursts.

- Keep an eye on the weather. If it starts to look like it will get nasty, you should head back.

- Let the child have some control as to the pace and where you go (within reason).

- Teach children about the outdoors and nature, and teach the Leave No Trace rules early on.

- Kids can get bored, so be creative: Spot blazes on trees, count squirrels, skip rocks, sing, create a scavenger hunt, and maybe even geocache.

- Teach kids how to read a map or even a GPS trail app.

- Take snack breaks and rest, especially if you have a slowpoke.

- If you have multiple kids in a group, pick a leader and then rotate the leadership. Kids love feeling in charge.

- Use positive reinforcement about how well the child is doing on the trail.

PETS AS COMPANIONS

- Responsible pet owners and well-behaved pets are welcome to hike on many trails. The first thing to check is whether the trail allows pets. There are parks that do not allow pets on hiking trails or boardwalks.

- If a trail requires a leash, don't just bring a leash—use it. Not only is it hiking etiquette, but it is also about health and safety. You may think you have the best-behaved, most mild-mannered pet in the world. But on a trail, around strangers, a pet could do anything. You do not want that on your conscience, do you?

- Know your pet. Is it fit for the trail? Is it in good enough shape for the demands of a hike?

- If you have concerns or want expert advice, check with your veterinarian.

- Make sure your pet is up to date on vaccinations before going on the trail. Fleas, ticks, and waterborne pathogens can cause serious illness. Talk to the vet about what you have planned and protect your pet.

- Teach trail manners, especially to young or untrained pets. You are bound to pass other hikers on the trail, so you need to make sure your pet is used to seeing other people and animals. You have to maintain control of your pet at all times. You also need to be able to keep your pet calm as other people and animals pass by.

- Pick an appropriate trail. Start small and build up the pet's stamina.

- Be aware of any trail hazards. Consider water safety, heat or cold, creatures, plants, and pathogens.

FUN FACT

Over 99 percent of the animals on Earth are smaller than human beings—and most are invertebrates.

- As a rule, keep a dog on a 6-foot leash. Be mindful of aggressive behavior. If your pet is reactive to new spaces, new people, being on a leash, or to other things—like people with hats or hikers with trekking poles—consider leaving your pet at home.

- Step off the trail to yield the right-of-way to hikers, horses, and bicycles.

- Bring extra water and a snack because pets will get thirsty and even hungry during the hike.

- Give your pet a nice treat at a resting point on the trail.

- Check your pet often on the hike and take frequent water breaks. If a dog is excessively panting, drooling, or vomiting, move to a cooler area and give it water.

- Use Leave No Trace principles and pick up after your pet; dispose of the waste properly when you leave.

- Stay safe around wildlife by keeping your pet away. A domestic pet can get or give diseases to other wildlife.

- For experienced hiking dogs, you may consider a dog pack for their water bowl and food.

- For experienced hiking cats, you can use a special pet backpack that lets them safely be carried and view the scenery.

HIKING GROUPS OR CLUBS

- Hiking groups and clubs are a great way to find kindred spirits and new friends who also enjoy outdoor adventure.

- Finding the right group or club can be one of the best things you can do to improve your experiences on the trail. It expands your hiking lifestyle to belong to an association of outdoorspeople.

- Most group and club outings are planned for the weekends.

- There are specialty clubs, like women's hiking groups, that may have outings during the week.

- The internet is a great place to start (search "hiking group" and "hiking club").

- There might be something local or in your county, but even if you have to travel an hour or so, hiking with a group or club is worth the effort.

- You can also check out Facebook groups, Meetup groups, American Hiking Society, the Sierra Club, the Ramblers, and regional groups and clubs like the Appalachian Mountain Club. These may lead you to local chapters and events.

- Note that there are some Meetup and Facebook groups you should be wary of joining: local singles hiking groups, "hunting for a good time" Meetups, gigantic metro area hiking Meetups, and night hiking groups. You want to hike, but you want to be safe, too.

- A further note on Meetup. If you are the organizer, you pay to use the service. Meetup offers very little privacy. Anyone can show up for a hike. People not in the community can see who has RSVP'd, so group members could become targets for theft while going for a walk in the woods.

- REI and L.L.Bean are outdoor outfitters that often offer group hiking events, as well as courses about hiking, backpacking, camping, and other outdoor adventures.

- Start your own group with friends and neighbors, with fellow gym members, through the local parks and recreation department or other community group, or on Facebook.

- To start your own group, get organized, formalize your organization, assign leadership roles, and publicize your group.

- If you lead group hikes, you have a set of responsibilities, including looking at the weather forecast, doing a recon of the trail, getting last-minute information or changes to the group, identifying group members who have first-aid kits and training, and identifying group members who have any special needs or concerns.

- If you have a trail in your community, a great way to protect it is to start a trail club to maintain a trail (or section of trail) and protect it from development. Just know that fundraising will be involved.

- Join a trail crew for a day, weekend, or several weeks. This type of activity puts you in touch with other hikers, but also allows you to volunteer to make trails better for everyone.

- If you are an experienced hiker, you can go on group hiking trips through organizations like REI, Backroads, Road Scholar, and OARS. The trips are classified by number of days and the activity level. Trip members need to make sure they qualify for the activity level, which is described in detail.

- Taking that a step further is the National Outdoor Leadership School (NOLS), based in Wyoming. With groups, you can learn outdoor skills, wilderness medicine, and more on extended wilderness expeditions and with traditional coursework.

DAY HIKING

- A day hike is any hike that takes a day or less, whether you go out for an hour or hike through a day, eating a meal or two on the trail.

- Be aware that there is a world of adventure as close as a nearby footpath. Many state and national parks offer broad networks of trails, as does national forest land. To find a day hike in your area, pick up a guidebook, ask at your local outdoor retailer, or check out websites like AllTrails or HikingProject.

- Start with local hikes and expand from there. You will learn a lot and get plenty of exercise just hiking a mile or two or three.

- Proper planning is important. Check maps and guidebooks. Know the trail distance, terrain rating, and estimated time for the hike. Keep a map and a trail app or GPS in a waterproof bag.

- Check the weather conditions and forecast.

- Know your fitness level and match it to your plan. You can prepare for hiking with strength-training exercises and/or yoga.

- The night before a hike, figure out the basics of what you are going to wear and take with you.

- To determine what you need to bring, first know how far you plan to go, how remote the location is, and what the weather will likely be. Longer and/or more remote hikes and possible weather changes may require more clothing, gear, food, and water.

- Bring the Ten Essentials, as appropriate for your hike. The exact items you carry should be tailored to your trip, but keep a daypack packed with the basics so you don't waste time getting out on the trail.

  - Keep a list of what you need on a day hike: footwear, trekking poles, hat, gloves, coat, bug spray, sun protection, watch and/or phone and/or GPS. Make sure your electronics are charged.

THERE IS NO SUCH THING AS BAD WEATHER, ONLY INAPPROPRIATE CLOTHING.
—SIR RANNULPH FIENNES

- A daypack with a cargo volume of 11 to 20 liters is perfect for a day hike.

- The most important piece of gear is your shoes. It is smart to swap out shoes at the start and end of your hike, too. If your feet feel hot or are hurting, remove your footwear, do a foot massage, and elevate your feet and legs during a break.

- Develop your layering system. You know your body and, depending on the weather, you know what will keep you at a comfortable temperature throughout the hike.

- Know that if you are going for a longer hike, you will need an energy snack and more water. A general guide is to drink 4 to 6 ounces of water every 20 minutes.

- After a few minutes of hiking, do some light stretching. Do it again on breaks and when you are done with the hike. This habit will improve your general flexibility and your recovery from hiking.

- Consider using trekking/hiking poles to reduce the impact on your knees. You might even take ibuprofen about halfway through a long hike if your knees tend to get cranky or inflamed.

- The world looks different at 2 miles an hour. Savor the experience. Don't make hiking into a project to lose weight, accomplish speed or distance, or move up in terrain ratings. You can keep track of your hikes—where you went and when, how far you hiked—for satisfaction and memories. But don't make a "job" out of the activity.

NIGHT HIKING

- To extend your opportunities for getting outdoors, look into night hiking, which gives you a very different perspective of the terrain and scenery. It is beautiful to gaze up at the sky when hiking at night. You can avoid hikers with dogs, and in summertime can hike without sunscreen and heat. You use all your senses, especially your hearing. This strengthens your connection with the environment and wildlife.

- Make sure you have an organized and complete daypack with the Ten Essentials. Bring layers for cooler night temperatures.

- The most important thing in night hiking is the same as day hiking: safety. You'll need to know when and how to use a flashlight or headlamp as well as other ways of improving your natural night vision.

- Bring a cell phone for emergencies and a GPS so you don't get lost.

- Tell someone where you are going, what time you are leaving, and when you expect to be back. Set up a check-in system so you do not disturb the other person's sleep.

- Especially starting out, take a buddy when hiking at night. Know yourself, and don't hike alone (day or night) if you get spooked when alone or in the dark.

- Start night hiking on a familiar trail. Head out before sunset and use the light of a full or nearly full moon if possible.

- Consider hiking in open areas with reflective surfaces like light-colored rocks. Slow down, because rocks and roots seem to come out of nowhere at night.

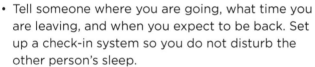

B• e ready for wildlife encounters. Again, going more slowly lets your eyes and ears be more aware of what is out there.

• Know that it takes up to 45 minutes for your eyes to fully adjust to the dark (why you start out just before sunset).

• By limiting the use of a headlamp or flashlight and relying on the natural light of the moon, your eyes will adapt to the darkness and your night vision will improve.

• Just like when driving a car at night, avoid looking directly at any light source. That affects your night vision, and you'll have to start the eye adjustment process all over again. If you encounter other hikers using headlamps and flashlights, look away or ask them nicely to turn their lights off as you pass.

• Never shine your light in someone's face. Be polite and turn off your light if other hikers are approaching.

• Your peripheral vision works better at night. So rather than looking straight at an object, try using more of an open gaze to cultivate awareness of what is above, below, and to the sides of your eyes and head.

• A brighter light is not always better for night hiking—it's tough on your eyes and significantly reduces your peripheral vision. If you are trail running or in an emergency situation, however, a bright white light is useful.

• Use a headlamp and/or flashlight that has a red light setting in addition to the white light setting. Your eyes are less sensitive to the longer wavelengths of red light. Also, look for multiple brightness settings (which helps with battery life, too). A headlamp should be comfortable but not bounce. A flashlight should be lightweight and easy to carry.

• Be extra cognizant of trail markers and blazes. It is easy to feel disoriented, even on a familiar trail.

LOCAL AND URBAN HIKING

- When you start out hiking, it is always best to explore locally first.

- The idea of taking a walk in the countryside for pleasure and recreation started in the eighteenth century.

- In the United States, Abel and Ethan Crawford cleared a trail to the summit of Mount Washington, New Hampshire, in 1819. The 8.5-mile path is the oldest continually used hiking trail in the United States.

- You will be amazed how many trails exist within 20 to 30 minutes of your home.

- Trail websites and apps like AllTrails, TrailLink, and HikingProject and online publications like *Backpacker* and *Outdoor Project* are great places to look for hiking trails near you.

- Local and regional hiking guides offer curated, detailed, authoritative information on the best hikes in your area.

- Your town/city's parks and recreation department and state parks department also have guides to parks and trails, directions for getting there, and maps.

- You'll aid other hikers by rating the trails you hike, writing reviews, and sharing helpful photos.

- Be aware of how current and recent weather conditions may have affected local trails. Rain leaves mud, snow can become ice, and wind knocks down (or loosens) trees and branches.

- Hiking is defined as a long, vigorous walk, usually on trails or footpaths in the countryside. The term "walking" is used for shorter, urban walks, but there is no reason you can't call it urban hiking.

- Other words for hiking are bushwalking, hillwalking, rambling, tramping, and just plain walking. Trekking refers to multiday hiking, and thru-hiking is long-distance trail hiking.

FUN FACT

"Tramping" is a term for overnight hiking/ backpacking in New Zealand and parts of Europe.

- Your first urban hike could be accomplished by jumping on local transit, taking it to a destination, then hiking back to your home. Unlike established trails, there are as many ways to get from Point A to Point B as there are streets in the city.

- Whether you are walking in a park, down city streets, or through a different neighborhood, a lot of urban hiking requires similar preparation and stamina. You are on a creative adventure, looking to discover new things.

- Urban hiking is a walk in a city or town that includes a sense of adventure as you wind through parks, climb stairwells, cross intersections, and meander through a city's obstacles.

- Sometimes you just want to get outside and may not want or be able to drive to a trailhead. There's plenty of nature in urban areas. Sidewalks, speed bumps, stairs, and curbs become your obstacles. You might not have to look much farther than out your front door for a unique long-distance hike.

- You can do local hikes with friends, family, neighbors, or by yourself.

- The focus of a local or urban hike is discovering adventure, not the number of steps or miles you complete.

HAPPY TRAILS TO YOU, UNTIL WE MEET AGAIN.
—DALE E. ROGERS

HIGHER-ELEVATION HIKING

- There are some important things to know about the environment at high elevation and how it affects the body and mind. You want the experience to be safe and enjoyable, not miserable.

- Hiking at higher elevations is worth it for the beautiful views and fresh mountain air, if you are properly prepared.

- Humans perform best, physically and mentally, at sea level, where the atmospheric pressure is 1 atm. Once you reach around 7,000 feet above sea level, the atmospheric pressure and percentage of oxygen decreases at a rapid rate, so it is much harder to breathe.

- High altitude is considered 4,900 feet above sea level. Very high altitude starts at 11,500 above sea level. Extreme altitude is 18,000 feet and above.

- With the thin air comes a lack of moisture, so hiking at higher elevations can be rough on the skin. You will need to drink more water, apply extra sunscreen, and wear clothing, hat, and sunglasses with enough coverage. Lip balm is also needed.

- Air temperature drops about 3.5 degrees F for every 1,000 feet of elevation gain. A 75-degree day at 5,000 feet will be 60 degrees at 10,000 feet.

- At higher elevations, you must move at a slower pace, breathe deeply, hike with an even stepping rhythm, and take breaks.

- In the mountains, summer weather can change drastically in a matter of minutes or hours. Plan your hiking on annual average temperatures for the destination.

- In August and September, afternoon thunder and lightning storms are common. Consider an alpine start, which means hitting the trails as early as possible. Always prepare for worst-case scenario with the weather.

- Flora and fauna also change at higher elevation. The altitude of tree line—the upper limit of where trees can grow—varies by climate and area. Harsh conditions at these higher altitudes mean that trees and plants are incapable of growing. The terrain becomes more rugged, so it is smart to have hiking boots with ankle support. Often cairns mark the route instead of a well-marked trail.

- It's even more important to strictly adhere to Leave No Trace principles in higher elevations.

- Above the tree line, there is little or no protection when bad weather hits. Ideally, head back *before* that happens.

- When you first notice any breathlessness, take deeper breaths and smaller steps until you have a sustainable pace again. On steeper sections, deliberately place each foot and take a breath with every step.

- Altitude sickness can occur when your body has not had adequate time to acclimate to the environment, change in atmospheric pressure, and lack of oxygen. It can be very dangerous when you climb to higher elevations too quickly.

- The symptoms of altitude sickness can include nausea, headache, lack of hunger or thirst, lack of coordination, difficulty breathing, confusion, and vomiting, and risks include brain damage or pulmonary or cerebral edema.

- Altitude sickness can occur even if you give yourself time to acclimate and even if you have spent time at high altitudes previously.

- The only way to deal with altitude sickness is to descend to a lower elevation (at least 1,500 feet), rest or reduce exertion, hydrate, and eat carbohydrates. Altitude medication may help. Call 911 for evacuation.

PLACES TO HIKE

- National, state, and local parks

- Forests and forest reserves

- Nature and wildlife reserves

- Wilderness areas

- Woodland trails

- Mountains

- Deserts

- Temperate rain forests

- Coastal paths

- Moorland

- Outback and bush

- Arctic and subarctic areas

- Exotic locales for vacationers

- Developed trails

- Social trails, mainly at camp areas

- Boot paths, way trails, and scramble paths formed naturally by years of foot or hoof travel

- Unmaintained, primitive, and abandoned trails that were once part of an official or maintained trail system (but respect trail closures)

IN MY AFTERNOON WALK I WOULD FAIN FORGET ALL MY MORNING OCCUPATIONS AND MY OBLIGATIONS TO SOCIETY.
—HENRY DAVID THOREAU

LONG-DISTANCE HIKING

- After some experience day hiking, you may aspire to a hike over a weekend or a week, generally referred to as backpacking.

- When you have accomplished a number of weeklong trips, you may want to tackle a long-distance hike, generally referred to as thru-hiking—an end-to-end backpacking trip on a long-distance trail.

- Completed trails in the United States include the Appalachian Trail (AT), Pacific Crest Trail (PCT), Continental Divide Trail (CDT), and John Muir Trail (JMT); trails under development include the Great Eastern Trail, Great Western Trail, New England Trail, Robert Frost Trail, Ice Age Trail, and *many* others.

- Consider how much time you can afford and invest in a thru-hike. Maybe you do not have five months, so pick a shorter trail that takes less than a month.

- Also consider section hiking, which is doing a single section of a classic thru trail. The John Muir Trail is a 211-mile stretch of the PCT, and it is spectacular.

- You can accomplish a feat like the AT, PCT, or CDT through section hiking over several hiking seasons.

- You will be off work and without a paycheck for the time you are on the trail. Expenses include gear and food, and you should figure out a budget for this financial challenge.

FUN FACT

Starting in the 1970s, low-impact principles made their way into most hiking and backpacking guides, the Boy Scouts, and the National Outdoor Leadership School.

- If going solo, you need to be comfortable with your own company, with solitude, with loneliness. There will be many mental challenges. The best way to prepare is to do some solo trips beforehand.

  - Between the large number of miles and total elevation gain, you know there will be physical challenges, including blisters, injuries, altitude sickness, and possibly Lyme disease. You will need to prepare for all of these and likely have to overcome at least some of them.

- You can train to an extent, but you can't train up to 20-mile trail days. You need to be in good shape, but not worn out by training. Go on a lot of backpacking trips before your thru-hike. Your feet will thank you for toughening them up.

- Take a first-aid course and wilderness medicine course.

- Most experts say you should set aside even more planning time than actual hiking time. It should be exciting to spend eight-plus months figuring out an itinerary, obtaining the necessary permits, arranging transportation to and from trailheads, estimating your average daily mileage, setting up resupply stops, and planning for contingencies when weather, injuries, and other things put a wrinkle in your plan.

  - Food is a major planning challenge, and your water needs are equally important.

  - As a backpacker, you probably already have a lot of the things you will need. Putting together what you want for a trip like this requires research and introspection. You should also test gear for a thru-hike during your preparatory backpacking trips.

THIS LIFE IS YOURS. TAKE THE POWER TO
CHOOSE WHAT YOU WANT TO DO AND DO IT WELL.
TAKE THE POWER TO LOVE WHAT YOU WANT IN
LIFE AND LOVE IT HONESTLY. TAKE THE POWER
TO WALK IN THE FOREST AND BE A PART OF
NATURE. TAKE THE POWER TO CONTROL YOUR
OWN LIFE. NO ONE ELSE CAN DO IT FOR YOU.
TAKE THE POWER TO MAKE YOUR LIFE HAPPY.
—SUSAN POLIS SCHUTZ

- Lightweight but robust gear is paramount. The weight of what you carry and your gear's ability to withstand wear and tear makes all the difference over hundreds or thousands of miles.

- Remember that you can swap out seasonal gear at resupply stops along the way.

- Most important: footwear. Some thru-hikers love trail runners and others want full-leather boots, but you are probably going to go through more than one pair. Make absolutely sure that all shoes and boots are broken in before the start of the trip.

GEOCACHING AND ORIENTEERING

- Geocaching is an outdoor recreational activity in which participants use a GPS receiver or mobile device and other navigational techniques to hide and seek containers called geocaches (or caches) at specific locations marked by coordinates. It is a modern-day treasure hunt.

- Orienteering is an outdoor recreational activity in which participants use a specially prepared orienteering map and compass to navigate from point to point in diverse, often unfamiliar, terrain while moving at speed. It is a timed event.

- A cache might be trinkets, a logbook and pen/pencil, or a disposable camera put in a weatherproof box and hidden.

- The geographic coordinates of caches are posted on websites for fellow geocachers to follow. The caches use a 5-star system to rate the level of difficulty and terrain. The website geocaching.com is the place to start—it has 3 million cache coordinates.

- Geocaching uses the skills of problem- and puzzle-solving. You will learn navigation, and a basic GPS unit is all you need.

- Basic geocaching guidelines include not placing caches on private land without permission or in national parks or wilderness areas. As with hiking, do not cross private property to reach a geocache without permission from the landowner. A cache should not include offensive material. Follow Leave No Trace principles.

- There are more rules of etiquette and lots to learn about how to play. Research ahead of time and connect with experienced geocachers.

- To go geocaching, you will need a GPS receiver, topographical map, and compass. Supplement with a camera, notebook, and pen.

- Cache finders leave behind a little token and take one as a souvenir. Cache treasures should be small, lightweight, environmentally and culturally friendly, inexpensive, and non-biodegradable. Toy cars, plastic action figures, or marbles are good examples.

- Orienteering is navigating through a series of checkpoints as a timed event. The route is not marked; it is up to each participant to figure out the best route on the run. The courses used for orienteering vary in length and difficulty, from beginner to expert.

- The goal is to find pre-placed control markers using a topographic map and compass. GPS is not allowed. Many participants are trail runners.

- Orienteering clubs put on meets and provide training—check out Orienteering USA's website, REI and L.L.Bean, and parks and recreation departments.

- Both geocaching and orienteering require sturdy outdoor footwear, appropriate clothing and layers for the weather, and a safety whistle. Carry some of the Ten Essentials, especially on a several-hour or multiday orienteering event.

- An orienteering map is a topographic map that is customized to cover the meet area in great detail. You'll need to be very familiar with this type of map and its many symbols.

- Every orienteering course has a series of controls where you record your visit. Some meets have a simple paper punch hanging from the control markers, but many now use controls that you "punch" electronically by inserting an "e-punch" timing stick. These are usually rented from the registration table.

- As with geocaching, there is lots to learn about orienteering before getting started. Make sure you're comfortable with the basics before heading out on your own.

- Remember that both of these activities are designed to be fun, even if there is a competitive aspect. It's an extension of hiking and running in nature.

SCAVENGER HUNTS FOR THE TRAIL

- The features of your planned trail will help determine what to incorporate in the scavenger hunt.

- Make a list of the items that would most likely be found in that area.

- Flora: berries, bird's nest, blade of grass, clover leaf, dark or light green leaf, dead tree, dew on a flower or leaf, different shades of green or brown, eroded soil, fern, fungus on a tree, grain of sand, hole in a tree, leaf with insect holes, moss, mud, pinecone, pine needles, pine tree, poison ivy, rocks with colors, seeds or seedpod, signs next season is coming, small pebble, smooth or shiny rock, tree with blossoms, unusually shaped leaf, wildflowers, Y-shaped twig.

- Fauna: ant, beetle, bird, butterfly or moth, caterpillar, deer, deer tracks, evidence of the presence of animals, evidence of the presence of people, insects on a tree, ladybug, lizard, spiderweb, squirrel, worm.

- In a deciduous forest, find an acorn, dandelion, deer tracks, helicopter maple seed, human trash item you can recycle, oak leaf, aspen bark, raccoon tracks, etc.

- The items don't necessarily have to be "found," but can be experiential: catch a fish, cross a creek bed, hang from a low tree branch, hear a birdsong or call, hike to the top of a hill, skip a rock, spot a squirrel, etc.

- Try an alphabet hike: Find items with names that begin with each letter of the alphabet, going in order from A to Z.

- Listen for/to: animals rustling, bees buzzing, birds singing, crickets chirping, leaves underfoot, running water, wind in the trees.

FUN FACT

The sights, sounds, and smells of nature calm activity in a part of the brain that research has linked to mental illness. Nature seems to also reduce the mind's propensity to ruminate, which is linked to anxiety and depression.

- Feel: plant leaves (nonpoisonous!), rotten wood, texture of various rocks, tree bark, wet mud, wind blowing on your face.

- Smell: cedar, flowers, fresh air, green grass, mud, pines.

- Watch: animals in their homes/shelters or eating, ants moving something, clouds going by, fish jumping, leaf falling to the ground, lightning bugs, reflections in water, something funny, something unusual, spiderweb with insect, stars in the sky, sunlight coming through trees, sunrise or sunset, wind blowing the leaves.

- Have a scavenger hunt using a camera, taking pictures of the items on the list.

- Bring along paper and pencil for a leaf rubbing on the hunt. Set an interesting leaf on a hard surface like a flat rock and hold a piece of blank paper in place on top. Gently shade over the leaf and surrounding area with the pencil to create an image of the leaf's shape and texture.

- Identify foods that are eaten by various animals while on the hunt.

- Play the game Twenty Questions or What Am I? instead of or in addition to the hunt.

- Draw a picture of an animal, bird, butterfly, flower, or tree.

- Identify different types of birds, flowers, leaves, plants, or trees.

- Write a story about what you saw, smelled, heard, and felt on the hike.

VOLUNTEER TRAIL WORK

- Give back to the trails you enjoy. You can donate your time to help maintain your favorite trails and recreation spots.

- Trail work is great for the environment, and it is another chance for you to get outside. Crews improve the trails (and thus the hiker experience) and reduce impacts to natural resources along trail corridors.

- The work is usually seasonal, such as from May through October. Projects last for a day, weekend, or week or more.

- Trail work includes checking on the trail's condition, clearing drainage areas, lopping (trimming) the corridor, digging new trails, sawing tree blowdowns, setting stone steps, and other small and larger projects. Trail work is hard physical labor that involves working with hand tools and getting dirty.

- Crews may work an 8-hour day, rain or shine, regardless of insects. Trail workers often hike a number of miles each day, carrying their tools and gear.

- All crew members are expected to participate equally in routine tasks such as cleaning, cooking, and tool care.

- Accommodations vary, from backcountry tent camps to tenting in developed campgrounds to cabins accessible by vehicle.

FUN FACT

Since the National Trails System was established in 1965, it has grown to include 30 National Scenic and Historic Trails and over 1,000 National Recreation Trails for a total of more than 50,000 miles.

- Consider your backpacking and camping experience when deciding what you can handle as a volunteer trail worker.

- Crew members must be able to work and live cooperatively and in close proximity with fellow volunteers of all ages, genders, and nationalities.

- There are trail projects and volunteer trail crews set up for sections that need work on major trails, like the Appalachian Trail and Pacific Crest Trail.

- The Appalachian Mountain Club has weekend trail work parties, teen trail crews, and professional trail crews. There is also an Adopt-a-Trail program in New Hampshire, New Jersey, and Maine, where volunteers take ownership of a section of specific trail and oversee basic maintenance of that trail. Trail organizations in other states offer similar programs.

- The American Hiking Society works with organizations and nonprofit groups through its Volunteer Vacations program.

- The National Park Service has a Volunteers-in-Parks program. It offers free national park access once you have volunteered for 250 hours.

- Western US organizations to check into include the Pacific Crest Trail Association (CA, OR, WA), Wildlands Restoration Volunteers (CO, WY), The Trail Center (northern CA), and the Arizona Trail Association.

- Eastern US organizations besides the Appalachian Mountain Club are the Green Mountain Club (VT), Appalachian Trail Conservancy (East Coast), Florida Trail Association, and more.

- REI has volunteering classes and events. REI also teams up with the USDA Forest Service to set up stewardship workdays.

- There may be paid internship programs for college-age students in areas where organizations perform trail maintenance. There are also trail maintenance jobs with state and national parks organizations.

PREPARATION AND PLANNING

MAY YOUR TRAILS BE CROOKED, WINDING,
LONESOME, DANGEROUS, LEADING TO THE
MOST AMAZING VIEW. MAY YOUR MOUNTAINS
RISE INTO AND ABOVE THE CLOUDS.
—EDWARD ABBEY

HIKING BEGINS BEFORE YOU REACH THE TRAILHEAD. IT might seem fun to jump into the car spontaneously and hike a favorite trail, but that is not a wise move. The preparation and planning for hiking, like for so many other activities, is just as important as the activity itself.

Your health and safety depend on what you wear and pack for your hike. Anything can happen when you are miles away from your vehicle or stopping place. Weather forecasts can be off, or change, too.

This chapter gives you lots of information about getting ready, what to eat and drink, and what to take and wear. But this is just an introduction. Consult experts, outdoor shops, and resources for all things gear before you make a big purchase or head out for a trek. There is a *lot* to know about clothing, shoes, and other gear that is not included in this book.

FUN FACT

Regional hiking associations in the United States include the Adirondack Mountain Club, Appalachian Mountain Club, Colorado Mountain Club, Florida Trail Association, Green Mountain Club, The Mountaineers, NY-NJ Trail Conference, Potomac Appalachian Trail Club, Sierra Club, Wasatch Mountain Club, and others.

PRE-SEASON

- Set your goals and expectations.

- Research terrain, climate, and challenges.

- Create a day-hike checklist. Create any other checklists you could use.

- Walk with your backpack or daypack.

- Break in your hiking footwear.

- Test your clothing.

- Test your hardware. Break it in. Make repairs.

- Pack your gear. Make sure you have the Ten Essentials.

- Exercise/work out.

- Stretch.

- Spend as much time outdoors as you can before your hike, even in poor weather. Acclimate to the weather.

- Make sure your skills are adequate.

- Brush up on Leave No Trace principles.

- Know your limitations.

- Know what food and drink to bring.

- Be prepared to take rest breaks.

- Do not be afraid to slow down and alter your plans.

PRE-HIKE

- Check multiple weather reports.

- Choose a trail. Make sure you and your companion(s) can handle it. Study the map and print it out.

- Save the parking location on Google Maps or another app or website you use.

- Don't leave packing to the last minute. Have a daypack or backpack with the basics in it, ready to go anytime. The night before, go through your checklist and make sure everything you need is packed. Anything you can't pre-pack (food, water, watch), make a list!

- In fact, if you don't have a day-hiking checklist, make one!

- Choose your clothes the night before. Set them out near your pack, and also set out any other gear you will take, like trekking poles.

- If you need to clean or prep your footwear, do that the night before.

- Charge your phone, GPS, watch—whatever electronics you will carry.

- Make sure there is gas in the car if you are driving to the trailhead.

- Visualize your hike the night before. Check out photos of the trail online and then close your eyes and enjoy dreaming about the trail.

- What you eat the day before your hike can have as much impact as what you eat during the hike. Complex carbohydrates and protein are key, in combination. Go low on sugar because although you will get immediate energy, it will be followed by a crash.

- The day of the hike, eat a light breakfast 1 to 3 hours before you start. You need foods that give you energy and power, like oatmeal, eggs, whole wheat toast, yogurt, peanut butter, nuts, raisins, brown rice or whole grain pasta, fruits, and vegetables. You should never hike with an empty stomach.

- Pre-hydrate for one to two days before the hike, drinking around eight glasses of water each day. And even if you are not a fan of having to go to the bathroom during a hike, drink around 16 fluid ounces of water before setting out.

- Let someone know when you are leaving, where you are going, and when you expect to return.

- Stretch for 5 minutes within 5 to 10 minutes of starting out on the hike. Read up on dynamic stretching: active stretches that move muscles through their entire range of motion and are not held at the end position.

- With good planning and preparation, you can set your worries aside, have fun, relax, and enjoy the great outdoors.

- Take your time and explore at your own pace. When you are outdoors, there is no hurry. Take this opportunity to connect with your partner(s) and nature.

SPENDING A FEW HOURS—OR A FEW DAYS—
IN THE WOODS, SWAMPS OR ALONGSIDE
A STREAM HAS NEVER SEEMED TO ME A
WASTE OF TIME. . . . I DERIVE SPECIAL
BENEFIT FROM A PERIOD OF SOLITUDE.
—JIMMY CARTER

CHOOSING A TRAIL

- Choosing the right trail is not always as simple as it sounds. Be honest with yourself about your fitness level. Hiking is a full-body workout, but your legs and core/abdomen are taking most of the stress. If you hike above your ability level, problems can occur through exhaustion or injury.

- Can you walk or run a mile? Do you have ankle or joint problems? Do you have asthma, allergies, or heart problems? Be conservative. You might want to talk to your doctor before beginning hiking.

- Hiking trails are rated by elevation, surface/terrain, and distance in a very general classification system.

- An "easy" trail has little or no elevation gain and a well-maintained surface.

- A "moderate" trail has a steady ascent with some roots and other obstacles.

- A "difficult/strenuous" hike has steeper, longer ascents that likely include roots, rocks, and debris.

- The Yosemite Decimal System is also used in some cases: Class 1: an easy hiking trail with minimal elevation and almost no obstacles along the way; Class 2: a more difficult hike that sometimes requires you to place your hands on the ground or surrounding surface for balance; Class 3: scrambling or unroped climbing; Class 4: climbing with a rope; and Class 5: technical climbing.

- Steepness is the same as grade and refers to how much elevation you gain in a given distance. Beginning hikers should choose trails with a smaller grade, found by dividing the horizontal distance by the vertical distance. A trail that ascends 1,000 feet over 5 miles is less steep than a trail that ascends 2,000 feet over 2 miles.

- For elevation gain, add an hour to your estimated hiking time for every 1,000 feet up. High-altitude trails take more time because of the impact of elevation on your body.

- Crowd-sourced information on apps and websites is not always reliable. Look for an up-to-date hiking guidebook for the area for authoritative information. Trail mileage measurement in general is rife with complexities and difficulties. Be prepared for differences from what your sources report.

- If information about a trail on a website or other resource is more than three years old, try checking other internet resources or contact the local parks and recreation department for updated information. Compare information from various sources to get the most accurate, complete picture.

- The average time for hiking a trail does not account for hikers' physical condition, weather, traffic on the trail, and other factors. If the hike is long, then it is more difficult. If you are lagging in energy, it takes longer. Though experienced hikers walk 2 to 3 miles per hour, a beginner should plan on covering 1 to 2 miles per hour.

- Keep track of your hikes in a journal—length, difficulty rating, hiking time—for a helpful future reference.

- Start slowly as a beginning hiker or if you have not hiked in a while and are starting up again. Hike 1 mile, then in a week do an extra mile. Build up your distance.

- Start with only "easy" hikes. Remember that difficulty ratings are subjective. Do your research; some hikes rated "easy" might actually be "moderate" (or moderate to you).

- If you start out on a trail and it is totally different than you expected, or you are uncomfortable for any reason, stop. There are plenty of other trails, maybe in the same park or close by.

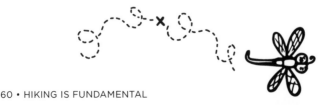

AVOIDING TIMES WITH CROWDS AND BUGS

- Hike in the middle of the week.

- Hike during the winter.

- Hike very early in the day in summer.

- Hike in the late afternoon.

- Hike at night.

- Hike in the rain or other precipitation.

- Find trailheads that are located away from main roads or parking lots.

- Hike backward, starting at the end of a trail.

- Seek out trails that receive less traffic or are under the radar.

- Hiking farther, longer, or higher helps you avoid casual hikers.

- Bug populations generally peak late May through June.

- Blackflies are most active in the morning. In many areas, activity peaks tend to occur around 9 to 11 a.m. and again from 4 to 7 p.m.

- Mosquitoes swarm at dusk and are also active during early morning hours before the sun has fully come up and the day is not yet hot. It very much depends on the temperature where you are hiking. But mosquitoes find daylight to be deadly, as direct sunlight dehydrates them.

- Mosquitoes and other bugs are attracted to fragrances.

- Mosquitoes are less active below 60 degrees F.

- Bugs prefer shade to direct sunlight.

- Winds over 5 mph deter bugs' flight.

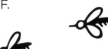

ASSESSING TRAIL CONDITIONS

- What is the purpose of the trail you have chosen to hike? Is it in a good or poor location? How would water, wind, or people affect that trail?

- Check online reviews of the trail. Are there problems brought up in the reviews?

- What is the rated difficulty of the trail? Be aware that hikers themselves rate the trails. See if there are reviews where other hikers challenge the rating that was given to the trail.

- Be aware of major events that could impact a trail, such as local flooding, ice storms, forest fires, and so on.

- Trails can also be closed for reasons that have nothing to do with hiking conditions, such as a pandemic.

- Pay attention to seasonal issues.

- Check your route to the trailhead. Are there road closures or detours?

- Certain hikes require more research and planning. If you want to do a hike that starts and finishes at different places, you'll need to shuttle vehicles to the start and end points.

- Many areas offer several types of hike, such as out-and-back and loop hikes. If the first trail you planned to hike has bad conditions, there are bound to be other trails to choose from—right there or nearby.

- Heavier than usual rainfall can cause rivers and streams to run high and fast, making them dangerous to cross.

- A drought may cause a usually reliable water source to run dry.

FUN FACT

In a forest the air is always slightly warmer in cold months and cooler in warm months than the air in surrounding regions (evaporation and transpiration control the temperature).

- A long, cold winter with heavy snowfall may result in trails that are blocked by ice and snow into late spring or early summer. Some trails won't be accessible in early spring if they are covered with snow.

- Trail conditions may vary considerably due to elevation, where sections are in relation to a mountain or mountain range, and exposure or non-exposure to sunlight.

- When following a trail that involves fording a river, bear in mind that after snowmelt, you may need to find an alternate route.

- A water crossing is one of the more common hazards on trails. Take your time. Cross where there is a bridge or something like it (fallen logs, rock-hopping) wherever possible. Be especially mindful of children and pets around moving water. Remember that you don't know the depth of any body of water you can't see the bottom of. Surfaces under the water are likely to be more slippery than you'd expect. Test rocks or logs before stepping fully onto them.

- If you come to a hazard, stop, think, and talk it through with your hiking partner(s). Consider the implications of taking certain actions. Then hike your own hike. Do not let others determine your decisions. Make your own evaluation with regard to your limits and experience.

- After every hike, evaluate your day on the trail. Think about the decisions you made and whether they turned out the way you intended. Would you do anything differently next time?

JUDGING DISTANCE AND TIME

- It is important to know your pace compared with an average hiker when planning a hike. Most guidebooks and trail apps offer an estimate for hiking the described trails. Know how long it takes you to hike a mile, but remember your pace will vary with elevation and trail conditions.

- Use a timer on your watch or phone and a map (or watch app) to figure out where a mile begins and ends. Taking natural steps, time how long it takes you to hike a mile.

- The variables that will affect this number include your fitness level, obstacles on the trail (roots, rocks, streams), weather, and the weight of your daypack or backpack.

- How long does it take to hike a mile? Here is an example: With 300 feet of elevation gain, at a slow pace, on an "easy"-rated trail, with a light pack—about 32 minutes minimum.

- You can also use an online hiking calculator to estimate your round-trip hiking time (moving time) based on distance, elevation gain, intended pace, trail surface, and pack weight. Northwest Hiker's hike evaluation tool is a good one and can be found at www.nwhiker.com/HikeEval.html.

FUN FACT

Map scales (1 inch on map to inches on ground): 1:24,000 is best for detailed route-finding, 1:62,500 is for day hiking on familiar terrain, 1:100,000 is only for planning, and 1:500,000 is for driving to the trailhead.

- You can also use Naismith's Rule to help with planning a walking expedition or hike. Allow 1 hour for every 3 miles forward, plus an additional hour for every 2,000 feet of ascent. It estimates hiking time on reasonably easy ground based on 19.5 minutes for every mile, plus 30 minutes for every 1,000 feet of elevation gain.

- Book Time is a system of estimating hiking time in the mountains based on 30 minutes for every mile, plus 30 minutes for every 1,000 feet of ascent. Book Time is commonly used in hiking guidebooks.

- The result of these calculators and calculating rules is usually considered the minimum time necessary to complete a route.

- A method for estimating distance is pace length. It is not as accurate as GPS, but it gives a reasonable approximation of distance traveled. First you measure your stride. A pace or complete stride is a measured two steps. A typical pace (two steps) measures about 50 to 60 inches.

- Develop a pace average on a controlled area before using the method to measure hikes. Measure the number of paces you take on a football field or track by walking the sideline. Or you can use a pedometer or pedometer phone app.

  - The pace average will only tell you so much, as the complexity of the terrain will impact stride and your average. You might also want to see what your pace average is on sloping ground, on soft and hard soils, and on smooth and rocky ground.

> NATURE IS LIKE A BEAUTIFUL WOMAN THAT MAY BE AS DELIGHTFULLY AND AS TRULY KNOWN AT A CERTAIN DISTANCE AS UPON A CLOSER VIEW; AS TO KNOWING HER THROUGH AND THROUGH, THAT IS NONSENSE IN BOTH CASES, AND MIGHT NOT REWARD OUR PAINS.
> —GEORGE SANTAYANA

- Many hikers learn to use a map and compass, both for navigation (and backup to GPS) and for estimating distance.

- You can follow your route on a topographic map, using a compass to take bearings of orientation points to get a location. Measure the distance covered using a ruler or piece of string and match the length of your string against the map's distance key.

- Plot your hike's course using Google Earth's "path" function instead of a paper topographic map. Zoom in as close as the resolution allows, choose the ruler icon, then the path tab, and click along your route. This is more for post-hike checking than tracking as you walk.

FUN FACT

By 2060, day hiking is projected (by the American Hiking Society) to see the greatest rate of growth in adults of any outdoor recreational activity.

FUN FACT

Conifer forest has the simplest structure, while deciduous forest has an upper and lower story of tree canopy—and a rainforest canopy has at least three layers.

- Track your progress with a GPS device or a phone app with a recreational GPS tracking system, especially for day hikes. For longer or multiday hikes, a dedicated GPS device is preferable.

- If you are limited by time, you will need to know how many miles you can tackle on the hike and ensure that the route you choose is within your time constraints.

- If you choose a destination with a fixed length, you must still decide how many miles you can hike depending on how much time you have and your physical condition as well as that of your hiking partner(s).

ADOPT THE PACE OF NATURE:
HER SECRET IS PATIENCE.
—RALPH WALDO EMERSON

CHOOSING CLOTHING

- Choosing clothes for a hike depends on many personal variables, as well as weather. Focus on function, not fashion. Here are some basic do's and don'ts.

- Cotton is generally a no-no for everything, from underwear to outerwear, head to toe. Cotton holds on to water, so it will keep you feeling hot and sweaty in warm weather and chilly if things turn cold and wet.

- Polyester, nylon, and merino wool work for all layers. They move sweat off the skin (moisture-wicking) and are quick to dry. Wool is not prone to retaining odors.

- One downside to synthetics like polyester and nylon is that they incorporate recycled materials that retain odors. Some garments have an antimicrobial treatment to neutralize odor-causing bacteria. Fleece is also polyester, and the thick fibers and chemical properties create and hold in warmth.

- Silk has very little wicking ability, and is not odor-resistant or rugged.

- Pants should be comfortable and sturdy. You need to be able to move freely, but the fabric should not get shredded or pricked by brush.

- Shirts should be chosen for comfort, too, though for a really sunny day, you might want a long-sleeve UPF-rated shirt with neck protection.

- Jackets for warmth can be polyester fleece or a puffy with polyester fill or water-resistant down inside. For rain jackets, look for something waterproof/breathable so it will block rain and wind but also let you sweat normally.

- Hats for sun and rain should have a brim. Gloves and socks are thicker or thinner based on the weather. Socks need to be taller than your hiking footwear. Gloves need to be insulated and waterproof in winter; mittens are warmer than gloves of the same material.

- For women, a pullover sports bra without clasps is best. Underwear should be non-cotton and non-chafing. A tank top or camisole can add core warmth on cold days or be an alternative to a T-shirt on hot days.

- Long underwear is available in lightweight, midweight, and heavyweight fabrics. A lightweight base layer can be worn under shorts for sun protection or warmth. It's your call whether to wear underwear under long underwear.

- With socks, consider the right height to avoid abrasion, cushioning (light, medium, heavy), fabric (polyester, nylon, spandex, merino wool—not cotton), and fit (snug, but not overly tight and where the heel cup lines up with the heel of your foot).

- Gaiters look like legwarmers and are worn over hiking boots and shoes. They keep debris, rain, and even pests like ticks out of footwear. There are also waterproof gaiters.

- Bug-protective clothing helps fight against ticks, mosquitoes, no-see-ums, blackflies, and other pests. Consider long sleeves, long pants, and other clothing items with built-in insect repellent, or choose bug-net clothing.

- Layers are your friend. Each clothing layer has a unique function, and you can add or subtract those layers to adapt to changing conditions.

- Look at what you can afford while considering comfort and durability. Durable pants are worth the money compared with inexpensive sweatpants, for example. Decide which items of clothing you'd like to be tough and last. Invest in good quality, but don't go overboard. If a really expensive jacket gets ripped, you will be very unhappy (although many high-quality gear brands offer repair services).

- In the Layering Basics section, you will learn about important fabric properties such as wicking, insulating, waterproof, windproof, breathable, sun protection, and waterproof/breathable.

CHOOSING FOOTWEAR

- Your shoes or boots matter the most. Footwear needs to provide support, protection, and traction, yet still be comfortable.

- There are many choices, from ultralight trail runner shoes to mountaineering boots.

- Going to a store that carries and even specializes in hiking shoes and boots will give you a lot of information. A good salesperson can tell you about shoe components (uppers, lowers, midsoles, outsoles) and factors (supinate, pronate) you need to consider.

- Hiking boot uppers can be full-grain leather, split-grain leather, nubuck leather, synthetics, waterproof membranes, or vegan and may also have synthetic insulation. A boot may have shanks or plates as internal support.

- Hiking boot midsoles offer cushioning, buffer feet from shock, and determine a boot's stiffness. There is EVA (cushier, lighter) and polyurethane (firmer, more durable).

- Hiking boot outsoles are rubber but may have additives to make them harder. Outsoles have a lug pattern and a heel brake. If you plan to do mountaineering or winter backpacking, check for crampon compatibility.

- From your experience with other shoes and boots, you will know whether you can handle heavier footwear or would be uncomfortable or experience problems with it.

- Hiking shoes are low-cut with flexible midsoles. These are great for day hiking.

- Trail running shoes are often chosen by ultralight backpackers or for long-distance hiking and thru-hikes.

- Hiking boots have mid- or high-cut ankles. These are for day hikes or short backpacking trips with lighter loads. They are usually flexible and require less break-in time.

- Backpacking boots are high-cut and have stiffer midsoles, and offer support and durability beyond regular hiking boots. These are for multiday trips deep into the backcountry and for anyone carrying a heavier load.

- Tall leather hiking boots can offer added protection from snakes in the desert.

- Know your size. Have your feet measured professionally at a store that sells and specializes in hiking footwear. You can use online sizing charts, too. You need a thumb's width of space between your longest toe and the end of the shoe or boot.

- Try on footwear at the end of the day because your feet normally swell a bit and will be at their largest then. Bring along any orthotics if you wear them. Wear your hiking socks. Spend some time walking in the shoes/boots in the store.

- If you shop online, understand the return policy. Consider a brand you have worn before. Whatever you buy, read and follow the manufacturer's instructions about care and use.

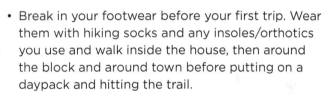

- Break in your footwear before your first trip. Wear them with hiking socks and any insoles/orthotics you use and walk inside the house, then around the block and around town before putting on a daypack and hitting the trail.

- Learn different lacing and knotting methods to adjust for the best and most comfortable fit. If your shoelaces are good and tight, your toes will not slam into the front of your boots when hiking downhill.

- Most important, listen to your feet. If you have a fit issue, return the shoe.

CARING FOR FOOTWEAR

- How long your hiking boots or shoes last depends on how many miles you put on them each year, the conditions you hike in, the footwear's durability, and even how you walk.

- Break in leather boots slowly. Let them shape and mold to your feet on a series of short hikes.

- When the outer leather of boots has gotten a little lighter in color and more pliable from use and sun, use a leather conditioner to keep the leather soft and hydrated.

- Use a stiff brush (boot brush, vegetable brush, or toothbrush) and water to clean off excessive dirt or mud, then dry the footwear thoroughly after each hike.

- Dislodge pebbles that are stuck in the outsoles. Another reason to clean the outsoles is to prevent transporting invasive species from one hiking area to another, or into your home.

- You can clean boots with a specialized boot cleaner, saddle soap, or a mild solution of dishwashing soap and water. Follow any directions provided for your boots.

- If there's a lot of mud, run the boots under a hose, scrubbing with a brush.

- Avoid salt water if you are near the ocean. It can rust the eyelets, which are hard to replace. If you get salt water on them, rinse as soon as possible.

- You can dry boots upside-down on a boot dryer or in a warm room. Never put the boots next to a heater or dry them in the sun. For quicker drying, try a fan.

FUN FACT

According to the *Journal of Experimental Biology*, hiking on uneven terrain increases the amount of energy your body uses by 28 percent compared to walking on flat ground.

- After each hike, no matter how wet or dry the footwear seems, remove the insoles and let dry.

- Stuff balled-up newspaper into each shoe for a few hours to absorb moisture and prevent mildew.

- Periodically spray inside your boots or shoes with an antibacterial shoe/foot spray.

- If boots have a liner, like Gore-Tex, occasionally swish a little clean water around the inside to clean the liner.

- Store footwear in a warm, dry place out of direct sunlight. Do not store in damp, hot, or unventilated places.

- If the footwear is leather, at the beginning and end of each hiking season, treat the leather with a waterproofing product to help them shed water and keep the leather from drying out. Waterproof the boots while they are damp for better absorption.

- Do not use mink oil or similar oils designed for industrial boots. It over-softens the leather of hiking footwear.

LAYERING BASICS

- Layering is the key to regulating your body's temperature comfort. There are many alternatives and options for each layer. Consider where you are going, what you are doing, and your budget.

- Know yourself in regard to body temperature and heat. Do you feel really warm when you are exercising and it hits 50 degrees? Or can it be 80 and humid and you don't break a sweat? The same with cold. Do you feel great when it is 25 degrees and a bit windy, or is that miserable and hard for you to manage?

- The base layer (underwear, T-shirt) you choose should wick sweat off your skin, which keeps you cool when it's warm and helps prevent you from getting chilled or hypothermic. For any clothing that touches the skin, a wicking fabric is best— polyester, nylon, other synthetics, or merino wool.

- Base layer weights are lightweight, midweight, and heavyweight.

- The middle layer is for insulation, retaining body heat to keep you warm. Thicker or puffier is warmer.

- Polyester fleece often comes in lightweight, midweight, and heavyweight (using the Polartec scale of 100, 200, 300, where the higher the number, the higher the loft of the fleece, and the warmer it will be). It stays warm even if damp, dries fast, and breathes well so you don't overheat.

- Insulated down and synthetics are compressible for packing. Down offers the most warmth, and its efficiency is measured in fill power ranging from 450 to 900. Fill power indicates the relative quality of down, with higher numbers denoting greater loft and insulating efficiency. Synthetics keep their insulating ability when damp; down does not. Both types are encased within a shell material that offers some water and wind resistance.

- The outer layer is a shell that shields from wind and precipitation.

- You are the best judge of what works for you. Most outdoor clothing is designed for a hypothetical average person who does not run particularly hot or cold.

- An example of cold-weather layering: midweight long underwear top and bottom, jacket with synthetic insulation, midweight fleece or insulated pants, waterproof/breathable rain jacket and pants.

- An example of cool-and-rainy-weather layering: lightweight long underwear top and bottom, lightweight fleece jacket, synthetic (acrylic, nylon, polyester, rayon, spandex) hiking pants, lightweight waterproof/breathable rain jacket and pants.

- An example of hot-weather layering: polyester underwear, short-sleeve synthetic T-shirt, synthetic hiking pants (long, zip-off, or capris), lightweight wind jacket. UPF-rated clothing offers added sun protection.

- Surprisingly, wool is best for not smelling when you sweat. Wool fibers can absorb large quantities of water vapor, helping keep skin drier and prevent the buildup of bacteria, sweat, and unpleasant smells.

- Most rain and wind outer layers allow some perspiration to escape, and almost all are treated with durable water repellent (DWR). Shells range from most expensive and functional to least: waterproof/breathable, water-resistant/breathable and soft, waterproof/nonbreathable.

- When the weather changes, adjust your layers. Throw on a shell at the first sign of rain or wind. Remove your insulating jacket when you start to sweat.

- To prevent extremities from getting cold, cover up. Wool and synthetic hats are good for winter, and you should cover your ears. A balaclava will protect your face in extreme cold.

- Fleece gloves provide basic warmth. Insulated gloves are better, especially with waterproof/breathable shells. Mittens, because they let fingers share warmth, are always warmer than gloves of the same material.

CHOOSING GEAR

- There are other items that should be on your hiking checklist besides clothing and footwear. Post a day-hiking checklist in a convenient place so you don't forget anything.

- A hiking daypack is the primary piece of gear for day hiking. It should hold 11 to 20 liters of gear for short hikes. For longer or more complicated hikes, you will need something bigger for more food, water, clothing, and gear.

- It is important to fit a backpacking pack to your torso length and hip size. A padded back and hip belt might be desirable for comfort.

- Daypacks and many backpacks have no frame, but some backpacks do. An internal frame with one or two stays (metal brace) will accommodate a heavier load.

- Pack access can be from the top, front, bottom, or side(s)—or a combination of these. Choose what is best for you. Sling-style or cross-body daypacks disperse weight differently and can be easier to access.

- Nearly all daypacks are compatible with hydration reservoirs and have water bottle pockets or an internal sleeve that can hold a water reservoir. Daypacks that include a reservoir are usually labeled as hydration packs.

- Backpack features include a suspended mesh back panel to keep your back cooler, a rain cover, a sleeping bag compartment, load lifter straps, and a sternum (mid-chest) strap.

- To fit a backpack, position the hip belt so the top edge is about one finger width above the top of your hips, then check where the shoulder straps fall. If there is a gap between the pack and your body, the pack may be too long for your torso. If the straps wrap more than a few inches down your back before they connect to the pack, it may be too short for your torso.

THE WILDERNESS AND THE IDEA OF WILDERNESS IS ONE OF THE PERMANENT HOMES OF THE HUMAN SPIRIT.
—JOSEPH WOOD KRUTCH

- Make sure you can adjust the hip belt loose or snug enough to fit comfortably around your hips.

- The pack holds food and water, navigation tools such as a map and compass or GPS, and the Ten Essentials, depending on your plans. The exact items you take should be based on weather, difficulty, duration, and distance from help.

- Trekking poles (sometimes called hiking staffs) enhance your stability and provide support on all types of terrain. Most are adjustable, and some have a shock-absorbing feature. They come with removable trekking baskets for snowy or muddy ground.

- Trekking poles come in a variety of sizes (varying in weight, height, and grip size), materials (aluminum or composite shafts; cork, foam, or rubber grips), and styles (adjustable, foldable, ultralight), with a variety of locking mechanisms (external lever lock, push-button lock, twist lock, combination lock).

- The Ten Essentials are covered in the "Introduction to Hiking." Absolutely essential is navigation such as map and compass, altimeter watch, GPS device, and personal locator beacon (PLB) or satellite messenger, as well as a first-aid kit, especially for foot care, with insect repellent, insect bite treatment, antibiotic ointment, and first-aid instructions.

- You should also have sun protection—sunglasses and sunscreen.

THE MOMENT ONE GIVES CLOSE ATTENTION TO ANYTHING, EVEN A BLADE OF GRASS, IT BECOMES A MYSTERIOUS, AWESOME, INDESCRIBABLY MAGNIFICENT WORLD IN ITSELF.

—HENRY MILLER

- A knife or multi-tool like a Swiss Army knife, firestarter materials, and an emergency shelter (lightweight bivy) need to be in the pack, depending on where you hike, the length of the hike, etc. A gear repair kit can be extremely useful in the backcountry and could include duct tape, cordage, fabric repair tape, zip ties, safety pins, repair parts for water filters, tents, stoves, and more. Instead of bringing a heavy roll of duct tape, wrap several feet of it around a water bottle or trekking pole. Rip off pieces as you need them.

- Extra water, food, and clothes round out the non-negotiable Ten Essentials.

- Extra gear to consider includes a headlamp (rechargeable ones are available), flashlight, camera, journal and writing instrument, binoculars, two-way radio, cell phone, and money.

ELECTRONICS

- A GPS device allows you to accurately find your location on a digital map. You can use a GPS app on a smartphone or get a GPS device specifically designed for outdoor adventures.

- Consider the basic specs of GPS devices, such as unit size vs. screen size. As the screen size gets larger, both the size and weight of the unit increase. The interface is either a touchscreen, touchscreen with buttons, or buttons only.

- Advanced GPS features include barometer/altimeter, electronic compass, wireless preloaded maps or third-party maps/software, memory and waypoint totals, geocaching features, digital camera, and two-way radio.

- A basic GPS device displays your position/coordinates and your position on its base or topo map, records your tracks (track points), allows you to retrace your steps, navigates point-to-point by giving you direction and distance to a waypoint, and displays trip data such as how far you hiked and how high you climbed.

- GPS units come with a software program that lets you manage maps, routes, and trips from your computer.

- Trail apps and hiking guides include maps based on GPS track points. You can search for trails near you, look up trail specs (skill level, accessibility), read and write reviews, and see and upload photos of the trail.

- Electronic topographic map layers display details in areas between landmarks. The trail is not as obvious as on a topographic map, but you will get an idea of the landscape in general, altitude changes, water crossings, density of trees, and landmarks.

- Sharing your location with others while you are hiking can be done with your phone or a dedicated GPS unit. This has pros and cons, of course, so think carefully. You can share your route with others after you have done the hike if you think it will help others find and enjoy the route.

- Charge your cell phone before you leave and monitor its battery power. Though cell coverage is growing and extending farther into wilderness areas, you can't count on having service in the woods. Put your phone in airplane mode when you are out of range to keep batteries from draining (they'll run down faster if the phone is looking for service the whole time). Personal locator beacons and satellite messengers offer much more robust coverage.

- There are battery-powered cell phone chargers that you can bring along on a hike. They also need to be charged before you go. To estimate how much capacity you need in a cell phone charger, figure out how many devices you are taking, the number of times you will have to charge each, and those devices' battery capacity. Pick a battery pack with roughly 1.5 times greater capacity than you require.

- Make sure you choose a battery pack with enough ports to charge as many devices as you'll need to charge at one time.

- Check the input and output rates for charging speed. If you expect to have little time to charge your devices, you will need a faster charger.

- Backpackers and campers on long trips often invest in solar chargers/panels. A solar energy producer is best used to charge a storage battery rather than the electronic device directly. This is because many solar chargers do not have circuitry to regulate the flow of electricity into your electronic device, which can damage the device. If you decide to buy a solar panel that comes with a storage battery, check the specifications to know if it will work for what you want.

- An altimeter watch uses a barometric sensor (to measure air pressure) and GPS data to provide an estimate of your elevation. You can use this to track your progress and determine your location on a map.

- If you use your cell phone, you should protect it with a case. Protection options range from simple ziplock bags or a zippered pocket, to soft cases, to smartphone cases, to hard-sided cases. You can consider weatherproof gear, too, like the Apple Watch.

- If your device gets wet, do not turn it on until it is completely dry. Try putting it in a container of dry rice or silica gel to absorb any lingering moisture. And if the device revives, back up its information right away, as corrosion may still develop later on.

- In heat and sun, keep your gadgets in the shade. If a device is exposed to dry sand or dust, blast it with a can of compressed air to clean it.

- If you do serious hiking, backpacking, or camping in backcountry/remote areas, consider a personal locator beacon or satellite messenger. Choose a PLB if you want to avoid subscription fees and are just interested in sending an SOS in an emergency. Choose a satellite messenger if you also want to send messages or want additional features like GPS navigation.

IT IS INTERESTING THAT IN BOTH
JAPANESE ZEN AND PLAINS INDIAN
ANIMISM, THERE ARE WALKING AND
SITTING FORMS OF CONTEMPLATION.

—ROB SCHULTHEIS

PACKING AND PRACTICING PACKING

- Your backpack or daypack can hold a lot of gear if you pack it smartly.

- Use your hiking (or backpacking) checklist. After you have collected all your gear, lay it out and plan your packing strategy.

- Remember, especially for newer backpackers and campers, you can save a lot of money by borrowing, repurposing, or renting gear. You can also learn what works best for you before making a large investment.

- Get the lightest (weight) possible versions of any big items you take backpacking. You can use handy packing organizers for separating items within the pack.

- Try different loading routines until you find what works best for you. Your pack should feel balanced when resting on your hips. It should not sway as you hike.

- The keys to packing are accessibility, balance, compression, keeping things dry, and fitting everything possible inside the pack (so you don't get caught on things or lose items).

- There are three zones for a pack: bottom, core, and top. There are also accessory pockets, and many packs have tool loops and/or lash-on points.

- Imagine that you are stacking a cord of wood, laying it down in rows (as opposed to columns). You can fill the nooks and crannies of your pack until you have a solid, stable load that is equally balanced side to side.

- Tighten the compression straps of the pack to streamline the load and prevent it from shifting during the hike.

- For backpacking, bottom-of-the-pack items are those items you will not need until making camp: sleeping bag, sleeping pad, sleep layers, camp shoes.

- The core should contain your food, cooking kit, stove, water reservoir, bear canister, tent (body, footprint, rain fly), and extra clothing.

- Any liquid fuel that is carried should be upright, below, and separated from food, with the cap screwed on tight.

- The top of the pack is for your insulated jacket, pants, rain jacket, first-aid kit, water filter or purifier, and toilet supplies.

- Different packs have different accessory pockets. Use these for map, compass, GPS, sunglasses, sunscreen, lip balm, headlamp, bug spray, snacks, water bottle, rain cover, keys, ID, and cash.

- Tool loops and lash-on points are for long items such as trekking poles, tent poles, large sleeping pad, camp stool/chair, ice axe, crampons, and climbing rope.

- Remember that just because you have extra space does not mean you should pack more.

- One of the most important things you can do in preparation is to practice with your gear. Besides practicing packing your backpack, this means setting up your tent and sleeping bag, using your stove and cookware, purifying water, starting a fire, going to the bathroom outdoors, and practicing good outdoor hygiene and cleanup. These can be practiced in the backyard or on day trips until you are ready.

EATING AND DRINKING DURING THE HIKE

- Even if you are just hiking for an hour, you need to have food and hydration options with you.

- When you exert yourself and sweat, your body loses fluid and electrolytes. You'll need to replenish both.

- You could eat traditional food and drink water, but you may want to consider energy foods and drinks, as they are portable, digestible, convenient, and have a long shelf life.

- If you buy energy foods and/or drinks, check the labels. Some are designed to be specifically consumed before, during, or after activity. There are bars, bites, chews, gels, sports drinks, and recovery drinks.

- The goal of eating during a hike is to maintain energy levels through a gradual rise followed by a gradual decline.

- If your stomach can handle solid food during activity and you'll be out for more than a few hours, bars (or energy bites and chews) with protein and fat give you sustained energy. If solid foods upset your stomach, try a sports drink with some protein.

- Drink water when eating energy bars, bites, or chews to make them easier to digest. Water is better than a sport/performance beverage, which may load you up with too many carbohydrates.

- Any type of candy or other high-sugar, high-carbohydrate foods will cause blood sugar to spike and then crash. That can cause post-trail depression and make you crave more sugar, so the cycle will repeat. Don't get on that roller coaster.

- To really discover what works for you during a hike, you need to get out there and experiment.

- A nutrition plan includes what you eat before the hike, too. Beforehand, it's mostly carbs and a little protein. During the hike, choose easily digested carbs and sugars (energy gels, chews, and fresh fruit). During a long hike, add some protein (energy bars, nuts, nut butters, beef jerky, and drink mixes that include protein).

- Even light exercise can deplete the body's percentage of water. How much you need to drink depends on the activity, intensity level, duration, weather, and your age, sweat rate, and body type.

- The general recommendation is 16 ounces of water per hour of moderate activity in moderate temperatures. You can fine-tune what you need from there.

- Keep water handy either with a hydration reservoir or a water bottle that is easily accessible. If you get dehydrated, the remedy is simply to drink water in sips. Adding a sports/energy drink can help restore carbohydrates and electrolytes.

- Drink smaller sips often rather than chugging infrequently. Drink water even in cold weather. You might want to set a timer as a reminder to take a drink every 20 minutes until you get in the habit of rehydrating.

- If your activity lasts more than an hour, consider replacing sodium, potassium, calcium, and magnesium with an electrolyte replacement sports drink. These are available in powders and tablets, too, for premixing with water before you head out on the trail.

- Water weighs a lot, so consider options like routes with water sources, looping back to your vehicle, or filtering water from a lake or stream.

- You can check your water intake by weighing yourself before and after exercise; you should weigh about the same. If you have lost several pounds, you are probably not drinking enough water. For every pound lost, drink 16 to 24 ounces of water. Increase your fluid intake the next time you hike.

POST-HIKE

- Even if you are in good shape, the first few hikes of the season or the first days of a longer trip can leave you sore and tired. Recovery is important, as is health.

- Be sure to brush off your clothing and footwear when you return to remove any insects and other harmful things before bringing the items into your home, even if you are going to wash the clothing immediately. Wash your outdoor clothing according to the manufacturer's directions. Make sure you close zippers and other fasteners to prevent their rough edges from damaging fabric in the washer or dryer.

- Food and drink after a hike aids recovery. Look for bars and drinks fortified with protein, amino acids, and other muscle-restoring elements. Eat within 45 minutes after finishing the hike, if possible.

- Protein helps your body rebuild tissue and recover. Complex carbohydrates and lean protein replenish lost nutrients. Examples: smoothie of low-fat milk and fruit, cheese with whole grain crackers, turkey wrap, yogurt with berries.

- Drinking after exercise gets your fluid levels back to normal and helps with recovery.

- Stretch after the hike. Time your stretches and poses; they need to be held for at least 30 seconds to have an effect.

- Tend to any injury or soreness you feel. Analyze your gear and footwear to figure out what may have contributed to the injury or soreness. Consider using a foam roller or other self-massage tool.

- After an intense hike, an ice or heat treatment can be beneficial. Cold treatments can help with inflammation. Heat treatments encourage more blood flow to tender muscles.

- Consider a contrast shower, alternating warm/hot and cold water. The purpose is to expand the blood vessels to flush waste products from muscle tissue.

- After your shower or bath, moisturize and exfoliate your feet. Looking after your feet will make you less likely to develop blisters, aches, or injuries.

- Clean and condition your shoes and dry them out. Clean other items you took on the hike, like your backpack and tips of trekking poles.

- Analyze the hike itself. Was it within your limits? Did you lose energy at some point or feel dehydrated? Did you start off too fast and not warm up and/or cool down? Smart hikers learn from each hike.

- Did you dress right for the weather? Did you carry too much or too little clothing with you?

- Did you use trekking poles? If you haven't tried them, you should definitely consider them. Using poles reduces the work that muscles supporting your knees and ankles must do. They help with balance and give your arms a workout.

- Sleep is important in preventing muscle pain after a hike. Give yourself the best sleep possible.

- If you experience stiff, sore muscles in the days following a hike, do some low-intensity cardio or low-impact exercises. Gentle movement can help stretch tight muscles, increase blood flow, and create other positive physical and mental effects.

- Unless you are on a long-distance hike, take a day off between hikes. Doing a different type of exercise helps your muscles recover and makes you stronger for the next hike.

- Don't burn yourself out hiking too much and then lose your enthusiasm or get injured. Balance is as important in physical exercise as it is in other aspects of life.

SKILLS AND FITNESS

DISPOSITIONS OF THE MIND, LIKE LIMBS OF
THE BODY, ACQUIRE STRENGTH BY EXERCISE.
—THOMAS JEFFERSON

WALKING AT A MODERATE PACE FOR 30 TO 60 MINUTES burns stored fat, builds muscle, and speeds up your metabolism. Walking can reduce your risk of heart disease, some cancers, diabetes, and stroke. As a weight-bearing exercise, it also helps prevent osteoporosis. Most walking and hiking is low impact, which means it causes less stress to your joints and body in general than high-impact activities such as running.

Why train for hiking? What skills do you need to acquire? You might think that there is not much to do to get ready to hike because it's walking, and starting out you will be hiking trails rated "easy." But if you have never hiked before, it is just like any all-new exercise: You should assume that training will be helpful, probably fun, and may prevent injuries.

Though you train for hiking by hiking, additional training really does help you get ready and stave off injury. An off-season or preseason workout plan that targets the muscles that support you on miles of trail—your core and leg muscles—increases strength and endurance. You can supplement that with balance and cardio workouts.

There are also physical skills you need, like basic pacing and rhythm, good posture, descending and ascending methods, crossing water techniques, and using trekking poles.

ESSENTIAL SKILLS

- When you become a hiker you also become a planner, a statistics analyst, a navigator, an environmentalist, and an improviser.

- Walking is simple, but as with any other exercise, good form is essential—starting with posture. Stand up straight and look ahead.

- Though beginning hikers look down at tree roots and rocks, they need to train themselves to look ahead. Looking at your feet or the ground puts excessive, unnecessary strain on your neck and back.

- Walk naturally and listen to your body. Are you comfortable with the way you are moving?

- Concentrate on taking shorter, quicker steps, but not too small. Understriding can constrict muscles. Overstriding, by lengthening your stride in front, can increase the force of your foot striking the ground.

- If you hear a flapping/slapping sound as you walk, you are not rolling through your steps properly. Your shoes may be too stiff—choose a pair that flexes at the balls of your feet. Or your shins may be weak and you need to strengthen them.

- Your arms should swing to counterbalance the leg motion. By using your arms effectively, you can add power and speed to your walk. Bend your arms at a 90-degree angle and swing them naturally back and forth, opposite your legs.

- Because you walk different trails or routes when hiking, it is important to vary your workouts, too. Start the season slowly, gradually increasing your mileage, but not more than 10 percent per week.

- You can gradually increase the pace and intensity of your hikes. Walking up hills and doing intervals are great ways to do this.

- At home, work with hand weights to create upper-body strength. This is part of the cross-training that allows your body to recover and help you avoid getting burned out on hiking.

- If you hike with more experienced hikers, imitate them. You must also develop social skills for hiking, like being aware of whether or not your companions want to talk, and speaking kindly to others you meet on the trail.

- Leave No Trace principles (see "Introduction to Hiking") are some of the most important skills any hiker can learn. This includes going to the bathroom in the woods.

- You need to know how to safely work with tools and gear, improvising when necessary.

- Navigation (see "Navigation" chapter) is an essential skill.

- First aid (see "Safety and Health" chapter) is an essential skill.

- Learning to deal with and respect weather and wildlife is also essential (see "Weather and Wildlife" chapter).

- Knowing when to take breaks, when to eat and drink, and when you should not continue a hike are part of the essential skill of knowing yourself.

- Practice makes perfect with all essential skills. Being ready for changing situations and possible problems will make you a much better hiker.

GETTING FEET READY

- Aside from swarms of mosquitoes or an ugly encounter with wildlife, nothing can ruin a hike faster than sore, blistered feet. There are ways to get your feet ready and care for them.

- Everything about hiking depends on your feet being in good condition and comfortable. Use quality gear. Don't cut corners on footwear or socks.

- Make sure your shoes fit right. The general recommendation is a thumb's width of space between your longest toe and the end of the shoe/boot. Some recommend that hiking boots be one-half to a full size larger than your regular shoe size. It might be best to be professionally measured and fitted. Wear your hiking socks when trying on footwear.

- New shoes are great, but always break them in by hiking around the house, backyard, block, or on short hikes. Do not keep a pair of shoes/boots that are too narrow, too tight, too short, or too big.

- Consider thin socks, as they have advantages over thick ones. Thick socks may increase sweating and they retain moisture, which keeps moisture in your shoes, increasing the chance of blisters.

- Always pack an extra pair of socks to make sure your feet stay dry and clean during a hike.

- Learn the different ways to lace your footwear. There are a variety of methods for lacing that can help minimize rubbing while giving your feet support. Examples include a surgeon's knot or runner's loop to keep your heel from slipping, window lacing that alleviates pressure on the tops of your feet, and toe-relief lacing to relieve toe-box pressure. Most kids learn to tie a granny knot, but learning to tie a reef knot can keep your laces tied and secured better.

- Toughen your skin for a few weeks before hiking season starts. Wear socks and heavier shoes when you go out or are at work. Then do short, gradually increasing walks or urban hikes.

- Strengthen your feet by walking barefoot, especially on uneven surfaces like sand. Do lower-body strengthening exercises and include your feet and calves. Good ones are heel raises, heel lowers, and towel grabs.

- Avoid ingrown toenails with proper trimming.

- File down calluses regularly. Exfoliate your feet and use a good-quality foot cream if you have any cracked skin.

- Tackle the threat of hot spots before a real problem (blister) develops. Consider using a quality lubricant to reduce friction. Stay away from powder or use it sparingly. It can clump and actually cause more problems.

- If, despite your best efforts, you do get a blister, take a few days off to let it heal with no friction. If you must drain it, do so with a sterile needle and keep the area covered to prevent infection and irritation. Most blisters will heal on their own once the source of friction has been eliminated.

- Wearing gaiters can aid in keeping debris from getting into your shoes. You want to keep your feet as clean and dry as possible.

- Hot, wet conditions inside hiking boots can allow fungus to grow. Use antifungal powder or cream to ward off the growth and spread of fungus.

- After a hike, roll feet around on a lacrosse ball or small massage ball to relax the muscles and improve foot flexibility.

- If you have foot problems and are planning to hike a lot or do multiday backpacking, consult a podiatrist. They may suggest orthotics and will help you get what works best for your problem and your particular footwear.

STAYING FIT IN THE OFF-SEASON

- Whatever your "season" is for hiking, when it arrives you will be raring to go. Make sure you stay fit in the off-season so you do not risk early-season aches and injuries.

- Make a list of all the different kinds of exercise you like and can do during the off-season. Mix it up on a daily basis.

- Turn some of your daily activities into training. While cooking, do stretches and yoga postures.

- Bike or walk instead of driving your car for errands or commuting.

- Walk to the grocery store with your backpack and fill it up for some practice.

- Walk to a nearby park to eat your lunch instead of staying inside at your desk or company break room.

- At home or at the office, use staircases for improving leg strength and cardiovascular fitness. Step-ups and step-downs do not require special equipment.

- Run or walk in sand if possible. It builds the muscles that protect your knees and ankles.

- Use trekking poles even for urban walks/hikes. If you are concerned about your knees or ankles, this could be beneficial, even in the off-season.

- Build your range of motion with exercises involving resistance bands or balance balls.

- Weight lifting has many advantages, from improving strength to staving off arthritis and osteoporosis through weight-bearing exercise. You can use free weights at home, as well as equipment at a gym. Make sure push-ups, squats, and lunges are part of your routine.

- If you don't usually hike in the winter, you could try snowshoeing or some form of skiing.

- Treadmills, elliptical machines, and stationary bicycles offer good workouts in the off-season or inclement weather.

- Add in other activities like yoga, Pilates, and martial arts. These keep you limber and help you avoid injury. Abdominal exercises help build core strength.

- Keep looking into ways to add exercise throughout your day. If you are really into exercise, though, it is sometimes tough to stop at an hour a day or take a rest day. You want it to be your "thing," but also know that overdoing it will hurt you. So go about adding in exercise in smart ways.

- On walks close to the start of your hiking "season," be sure to wear the shoes you will be hiking in—especially if you have not worn them for a long time or if they are new and need to be broken in.

WHEN YOU TAKE A FLOWER IN YOUR HAND
AND REALLY LOOK AT IT, IT'S YOUR WORLD
FOR THE MOMENT. . . . MOST PEOPLE IN
THE CITY RUSH AROUND SO, THEY HAVE
NO TIME TO LOOK AT A FLOWER.
—GEORGIA O'KEEFFE

ASCENDING AND DESCENDING

- It is critical to understand the concepts of ascending (going uphill) and descending (going downhill) on varied terrain. This lowers the risk of falls, stumbles, strains, and sprains. It also conserves your energy.

- In ascending, your body position should be standing tall with a straight spine and dropped shoulders. Avoid hinging at the waist, and position your pack in a way that keeps you from doing so.

- As you ascend, lean forward and keep your weight on your toes. With each step, extend and straighten your legs completely, but avoid overextension at the knees and ankles.

- Maintain a steady pace through the day, finding a rhythm between breathing and strides. This is especially important on long, gradual climbs over smooth terrain, where it is easy to get going faster than your lungs allow. The rule of thumb is you should be able to keep talking as you walk.

- As you ascend, loosen your backpack's hip and shoulder straps so they do not constrict your stride and breathing. Try to alternate the weight of the load between your shoulders and hips, which will minimize pressure on any single area.

- Shorten your stride on the uphill. Use your hands for assistance on high step-ups. Consider using trekking poles. If you are using one pole or a hiking staff, when ascending, step up with your stronger leg first and follow with the staff and weaker leg, using the staff to push yourself up. When descending, use the staff and weaker leg first to take weight off the weaker leg.

- Take rest steps with each forward stride: Straighten your knees to temporarily shift the load from the muscles to the joints.

- On regular terrain, use the standard heel-to-toe technique of walking. Keep your knees slightly bent on impact to keep the load on the muscles.

- When descending, there is a natural tendency to lean backward. Counteract that by keeping your center of gravity low and over your legs, which lets you land on your toes instead of your heels.

- Going down, you can pick up momentum, possibly more than you can sustain. Be careful and maintain a steady pace to avoid slipping and potential injury. Take short, controlled steps, especially on sand, scree, and wet leaves or rocks.

- On descents, tighten the hip belt and shoulder straps to minimize backpack movement so you keep your balance. In descending, you will feel the pack's weight on your back and shoulders more.

- Sit down and use your hands for balance on large step-downs. Place trekking poles in front to help you land safely.

- Use switchbacks (if available) or traverse a slope sideways to make the descent more gradual.

- Focus your eyes on where you want to go, not on your feet. Try a 45-degree angle or looking 8 to 10 feet ahead of your feet to start with. As your confidence and foot placement improve, you will learn to naturally look forward instead of down.

- It is better to walk slowly and take fewer breaks than to walk quickly and take a lot of breaks. Science says the body and brain go from activity stage to fatigue stage every 90 minutes, so on a long hike, walk 60 to 90 minutes and then take a 15- to 20-minute break.

- Keep your muscles in good shape and avoid injuries by stretching before starting your hike, during breaks, and at the end of the hike. Vary your stride, body position, and backpack adjustment whenever you feel tightness starting to build in an area.

- See "Hiking in Snow" (in the "Weather and Wildlife" chapter) for ascending and descending techniques on snow.

USING TREKKING POLES

- Consider using trekking poles, which can help you avoid falls, twists, and strains. Trekking poles or single hiking staffs are standard equipment for many hikers. They enhance your stability and provide support on all types of terrain.

- Features to consider include adjustability, foldability, shock absorption, weight, shaft materials, pole grip materials, and locking mechanisms (for adjustable poles). For hands that tend to get sweaty, cork grips are lighter and better than synthetic grips. They also change to fit the shape of your hand the more you use them.

- The right length for poles is when there is a 90-degree bend at your elbow when the poles' tips touch the ground. Check with your local gear shop or look online for measurement insight.

- If your hands tend to swell while hiking, using poles will keep them closer to the level of your heart, which improves blood flow to them.

- With each step, move the arm opposite your stepping foot and plant the pole with your step. If you get out of rhythm, lift both poles and reset, planting one pole opposite your stepping foot.

- Use your trekking poles to assess the stability of any rocks before you step on them. Use the poles to test terrain that is muddy or wet, and to brush aside vegetation, especially any that might be poisonous.

- Use the trekking basket attachment that comes with the poles if you will be hiking on muddy, snowy, or wet ground that may be slippery.

- Use the poles for negotiating obstacles, such as when you have to climb over a fallen tree or a small body of water. Use double pole planting for this. Place the poles firmly in front and then step over the obstacle—a mini "pole vault."

FUN FACT

Surprisingly, walking and hiking are radically different. Research shows that your joints, heart, and muscles perform in distinct ways during a hike compared with walking on a level surface.

- Double planting is also useful on steep ascents or descents where you need the power and stability, respectively, of both poles on the ground.

- When you are hiking uphill, you may want to shorten the poles about 2 to 4 inches for extra leverage.

- When you are hiking downhill, you may want to lengthen the poles about 2 to 4 inches, to extend them ahead of your body for extra stability.

- If you have poles with three sections, set the top adjustment in the middle range and then set the bottom to the length that puts your elbow at 90 degrees. If you need to make adjustments during the hike for uphill or downhill, you can do so using only the top adjustment.

- The right way to use the wrist straps is by putting your hand up through the bottom of the strap. Then pull down and grab the grip of the pole. This gives you support while allowing your hand to be relaxed on the grip.

- You can adjust the length of the strap so that when you bring your hand down on the strap, it lines up with where you want it to rest on the grip. Proper strap adjustment allows you to let go of the pole to take a picture, get a snack, or adjust your backpack and then easily grab the pole again.

- For hiking in urban areas, such as boardwalks and streets, add rubber trekking pole tips. That saves the tips of the poles for regular hikes and prevents scratching the pavement, rock, or other hard materials you are walking on. You and others will also not hear clacking noises on those surfaces.

NATURE IS PAINTING FOR US, DAY AFTER DAY, PICTURES OF INFINITE BEAUTY.
— JOHN RUSKIN

- If you choose to use a single pole or hiking staff because you have a painful joint or an injury, make sure you hold it on the opposite side to that joint/injury. Using the stick on the opposite side allows you to shift your weight more to the strong side. Move the weak or injured leg and pole together; this way each side of the body shares the load. As you step forward, the pole and opposite foot should hit the ground at the same time. Then step forward through the middle onto the stronger leg.

- Walk naturally and maintain a natural arm swing, as if you did not have poles in your hands. Keep your back as straight as you can and try not to lean too far to one side or too far forward. Only swing the poles as far in front of you as your legs would normally reach; do not overextend your arms. The poles may be angled slightly behind you so that as you plant them, you can push off to aid your forward movement.

PACING THE HIKE

- One of the most important things to do is hike at a consistent pace. Hikers waste a lot of energy by starting out too fast. In fact, you should stop to stretch about 10 minutes into a hike before settling into your pace.

- Muscles are cold and not happy with a fast pace right out of the gate. Speed on the trail does not equate to distance if muscle cramps and fatigue appear during the hike.

- There is a flip side. Starting too slowly and stopping to adjust gear, get a snack, look at the map, or chat impedes getting warmed up and into the proper rhythm for the hike.

  - On a daylong hike, and for beginners, start slowly—1 to 2 mph—which should feel easy. Then, after stretching at the 10-minute mark, start your sustainable pace of 2 to 3 mph.

- There are many factors that can affect your pace: trail conditions, weather, detours, and much more. If you have to go slower, so be it. Adjust your mental expectations. And, as you have learned elsewhere in this book, be prepared as much as possible before heading out on the trail.

- Take short breaks every 60 to 90 minutes and snack often for optimal calorie intake. Do some light stretching during each break.

- You can mix up your hiking stride. On flatter, well-maintained trails, using the same muscles in exactly the same way over hours (or days) will likely lead to injury. Try taking shorter and then longer strides. Get up on your toes and then back on your heels.

- Going uphill takes more effort, slows you down, and forces you to adopt a slower pace.

- Going downhill is harder and requires more balance, careful foot placement, and knee strength. Walking faster on the downhill to make up time will come back to bite you.

- To avoid running out of daylight on a hike, do not rely on the mileage on trail signs. Always double-check distances on a current map and with GPS.

- If you are exploring off-trail, your pacing will have to be readjusted constantly. One mile per hour is a good estimate for off-trail hiking.

- Add 10 minutes or more of stretching at the end of a hiking day. Focus on your calves, hamstrings, quadriceps, and glutes.

- Whether you are hiking 2 miles, or 10 or 30, aim to finish the day at the same pace you maintained throughout the hike.

- Be kind to yourself, know your body and mind's condition on the day of the hike, and accommodate any personal issues. Especially as you age, you need to heed your body's feedback signals within the first 30 minutes of hiking.

FUN FACT

Darby Field became the first Euro-American to take a hike with the purpose of reaching the summit of Mount Washington, in New Hampshire.

- If you "hit the wall" and every fiber of your being says "stop" or "slow down," be prepared to do just that.

- Log your mileage and time (speed) over one entire hiking season and see how it varies. Knowing how much distance you covered, divided by the time it took, gives you an average hiking speed for the hikes you have done.

IN MY ROOM, THE WORLD IS BEYOND
MY UNDERSTANDING. BUT WHEN I WALK
I SEE THAT IT CONSISTS OF THREE
OR FOUR HILLS AND A CLOUD.
—WALLACE STEVENS

HOW TO TRAIN FOR HIKING

- Whatever training exercises you do, adapt them to your body, not the other way around. If anything hurts, modify the exercise, swap it for another one that works the same area/muscles, or take extra rest days.

- Train at your own pace, slowly at first. Increase repetitions or add more resistance or weight as your training progresses.

- Always warm up. The best warm-up for hike training is a 5- to 10-minute walk.

- When exercising, inhale during the exertion and exhale as you return to the starting position. During faster/quicker routines, just make sure you are breathing normally.

- Rest for 30 to 45 seconds between sets of an exercise and 1 to 2 minutes between different exercises.

- Strength exercises to consider are jump squat, hip roll, step-up, heel down, squat curl with overhead press, bridge with hamstring curl, side plank with leg raise, hip clock.

- Other great strength exercises: sand walking or running, resistance band walks, balancing exercises, squats and lunges, leg curls, and push-ups.

- Training at home requires a simple set of dumbbells (free weights), a resistance band, maybe an exercise or yoga mat, a medium-size exercise ball, and a stable surface about 8 inches off the ground (training box, aerobic stepper, or flight of stairs).

- Cardio training is as easy as walking on a trail. Other options are outdoor biking, a stationary bike, and a treadmill.

- Before a long hike, plan for four to eight weeks of training with a mix of workout types.

CLIMB EVERY MOUNTAIN, FORD EVERY STREAM, FOLLOW EVERY RAINBOW, TILL YOU FIND YOUR DREAM!

—O. HAMMERSTEIN II

- Plan each week around two nonconsecutive days of strength training, two nonconsecutive rest days, and three nonconsecutive cardio training days.

- Do an hour of training, whether it is strength or cardio.

- Two weeks before a long hike, change your cardio days to long day hikes of at least 1 hour and up to 2 hours, with a pack close to the weight you will be carrying on the long hike. Add a fourth day-hike session on one of your strength-training days.

- On the training hikes, be sure to wear the same shoes that you will wear on the long hike. If you plan to take trekking poles, also use them in training.

- Hiking in the mountains requires extra strength and lung capacity. Training for higher elevations requires all the same gradual conditioning as for a long hike, but you'll need to start earlier—maybe six months ahead—to get ready for 8,000- to 9,000-foot elevations with a heavy pack.

- A thru-hike is a major commitment to long distances, day after day, for weeks or months. This requires mental as well as physical preparation. Most thru-hikers plan for at least six months, with a heavy emphasis on research. Shorter section hikes are often used in this type of training.

  - For a day or two before any long hike, do no training.

NORDIC WALKING

- Nordic walking is somewhat of a halfway exercise between walking and hiking. It is done mainly on paved surfaces.

- Nordic walking started in Finland in the early 1990s as a way for cross-country skiers to train in the off-season. It is a good off-season exercise for hikers, too.

- Nordic walking with poles boosts your stride and burns up to 46 percent more calories than regular walking. It strengthens and tones the upper body and core muscles and improves balance and stability. Using poles to walk helps reduce blood pressure, regulate heart rate, and improve oxygen consumption.

- You can work up to 80 percent of your muscles doing Nordic walking.

- Proper use of the poles and correct arm motion encourages good posture and works to overcome the hunching forward that people get from working at desks and computers, reading, and watching TV.

- The key to Nordic walking is using poles that are lightweight and have rubber tips for walking on pavement or other hard surfaces. You can buy poles specifically designed for Nordic walking that have angled rubber tips. But regular trekking poles with rubber tips can be used in a pinch.

- If you are walking on grass, sand, or dirt, remove the rubber tips for better traction.

- As with trekking poles, your height is key when choosing Nordic walking poles. Gripping a pole with the tip on the ground and the pole vertical, your elbow should be bent at 90 degrees.

- The angle and use of the arms and the angle of the poles is slightly different from using trekking poles for regular hiking. The poles are held close to the body, and the hands opened slightly as the poles swing from the wrist straps.

- Tighten the straps with each hand in the correct position around the pole, keeping the wrist straight. Your hand will then fit more snugly, making arm swing and hand control easier.

- Shoulders should be relaxed. The poles remain pointed diagonally backward and are not planted in front of the body.

- The arms and legs alternate. When the right foot is forward, the left hand is forward—and vice versa.

- The feet walk in a rolling motion, heel to toe. This lengthens the stride behind the body.

- Push the pole back firmly as far as possible with each step, the arm straightening to form a continuous line. The arm motion is loose and relaxed, and the force is applied through the strap. Keeping the arms relaxed and the poles behind the body are key to proper technique.

- The body is pushed forward past the pole until the pole forms a continuous line with the outstretched arm behind the body.

- The pole plant is between the front and back foot.

- As you push each arm past your hip, open your hand at the end of the arm swing. As each arm comes forward, pretend you are reaching forward to shake someone's hand.

EXERCISES FOR HIKING

These activities can complement hiking, especially during the off-season or on days when you do not hike.

- balancing exercises, such as tai chi
- biking
- running
- rowing
- stretching (especially quadriceps, calves, hamstrings, groin, back)
- walking
- yoga

These are examples of strength-training exercises that can benefit the muscles used in hiking. You can look them up in strength-training books, talk with a trainer at a gym, or seek exercise instructions and videos on the internet.

- back extension
- box jump
- bridge
- crunch
- dead-lift
- heel down
- hip clock
- hip hinge
- leg curl
- leopard crawl
- lunge
- mountain climber
- plank
- push-up
- sit-up
- squat
- step-up

To train for hiking, a basic plan might look like this:

- Week 1: Walk daily, starting with 0.5 mile and working up to 1 mile.
- Week 2: Walk daily, starting with 1 mile and working up to 1.5 miles.
- Week 3: Walk daily, starting with 1.5 miles and working up to 2 miles.
- Week 4: Walk 2 to 3 miles, 5 days per week.
- Week 5: Walk 3 to 4 miles, 4 days per week.
- Week 6: Walk 4 to 5 miles, 4 days per week.

- For weeks 4, 5, 6: Add in walking as you go about your day at home, work, in the garden, and doing errands.

You might also add HIIT (high intensity interval training) workouts to enhance your fitness for hiking. An example of a HIIT workout is 20 minutes of an aerobic exercise such as biking, rowing, running, or walking. Start with a 5-minute warm-up and then perform the exercise for 1 minute at 80 to 90 percent of your maximum heart rate (subtract your age from 220). Follow with 1 minute (more if needed) of recovery doing the same activity at an easy pace. The objective is to alternate high and low heart rates, repeating the segments ten times during the 20 minutes. HIIT can be training for hiking, as an off-season exercise, or as exercise you alternate with hiking ventures.

On a treadmill where you can program your walking speed, HIIT could work like this:

- Warm up 5 minutes at 3.5 mph.

- Walk fast or jog 2 minutes at 4 mph.

- Sprint 1 minute at 6 mph.

- Walk fast or jog 2 minutes at 4 mph.

- Sprint 1 minute at 6 mph.

- Walk fast or jog 2 minutes at 4 mph.

- Sprint 1 minute at 6 mph.

- Cool down 4 minutes at 3.5 mph.

NAVIGATION

THE STUDY OF THE TRAIL IS FASCINATING; THERE
IS SOMETHING PRIMAL ABOUT IT. AFTER ALL, WE
AS *HOMO SAPIENS* WERE BUILT AND PROGRAMMED
TO WALK. IF WE WEREN'T, WE'D BE WORMS.

—JAMES KLOPOVIC

WHEN YOU ARE WALKING ALONG WELL-MAINTAINED and well-marked trails, the only navigation skill you may require is the ability to locate your vehicle in the trailhead parking area. But there are times when you surprisingly get off the trail, or when conditions get bad and obscure the trail, or when you are just plain lost. Your safety may ultimately depend on your ability to navigate.

Even if you carry a GPS or a phone with a GPS app, the ability to interpret a map and navigate with a compass are fundamental skills every hiker should know. Basic information will be explained in this chapter, but you should supplement it by watching videos online, especially because sometimes a visual demonstration helps you learn new skills.

Also, there are great books about wilderness navigation, map and compass skills, and navigating using nature's indicators. You'll find some included in this book's bibliography.

FUN FACT

A large-scale map is 1 inch representing a mile or less; a small-scale map is 1 inch to about 15 miles.

NATURE'S INDICATORS FOR NAVIGATION

- If you lose your compass or your GPS/phone battery dies, how do you find your way back to civilization? You use nature's indicators.

- The sun's journey from east to west gives you one of nature's most accurate navigational tools. But nature's indicators, especially if you are new to reading them, are not infallible. Look for more than one indicator when trying to figure out direction.

- If you walk in the direction of sunrise in March or September and then turn around at the end of the day and head back toward sunset, you stand a good chance of finding your way back to where you set out from (out to the east, back to the west). If you walk toward sunrise in midwinter, you would need to walk with the sunset over your left shoulder to get back to the same spot at the end of the day.

- In the northern hemisphere, the sun will be due south at midday—the moment that the sun is highest in the sky (and vice versa in the southern hemisphere)—not what your watch says. The shortest shadow cast by a stick each day will form a perfect north-south line anywhere in the world, and this happens at midday. By marking the end of a stick's shadow tips over the course of the middle part of the day and joining them, a curve is made. The closest point on this curve to the stick is a perfect north–south line.

- You can create a shadow compass using a stick about 3 feet long. Place the stick in the ground and mark the location of the tip of the shadow. Wait 20 minutes, then mark the new location of the shadow tip. Draw a line between the marks; it runs approximately in an east–west direction. If you stand with the first mark to your left and the second to your right, you will be facing north.

- If you have an analog watch with hands, hold the watch out in front of you and point the hour hand at the sun. The midpoint between the hour hand and twelve o'clock is south (in the northern hemisphere; vice versa for the southern hemisphere). If you have a digital watch, stick a piece of paper with a clock face drawn on it and this might work.

- Plants can help indicate north and south when it is cloudy. In the northern hemisphere, most (but not all) growth will be on the southern sides of trees and rocks (vice versa for the southern hemisphere).

- Trees are never symmetrical and tend to be heavier on one side. The sun influences this and can be used to find direction. Looking at a tree from a few angles will help you see which side is "heavier," or the southern side, where the branches also tend to grow more horizontally.

- If you investigate the prevailing wind of the area ahead of time, you will also be able to figure out direction when you see exposed trees that show how the prevailing wind has blown them into their shape.

- You can create a makeshift compass with a small container of water, a magnet, and a needle, like a sewing needle, paper clip, razor blade, safety pin, or compass needle. Keep these items in your emergency kit for when your compass breaks. Magnetize the needle by rubbing it on the magnet twenty-five to thirty times. Float the needle on a leaf in water in the container (seashell, plastic jar lid). Wait and it will orient itself north to south.

- At night in the northern hemisphere, use Polaris, the North Star, to measure your approximate latitude. Point one arm at the star, stretch the other arm horizontally, and estimate the angle. Polaris is the tip of the Little Dipper's handle. First find the Big Dipper, then trace a line from the star representing the bottom corner of the Big Dipper's cup (farthest from the handle) to the top corner (farthest from the handle), straight onto Polaris.

- Celestial navigation differs between the northern and southern hemispheres. Some stars or constellations visible in one hemisphere could be invisible in the other. Crux, the Southern Cross constellation, can be used to locate the southern celestial pole in the southern hemisphere.

- The full moon and its movements across the sky can help you find your way, as the full moon basically travels the same path the sun does during the day. This method is only useful once a month, and then only if skies are clear.

- The crescent moon has "horns." When the crescent moon is in the sky, use something straight to make a line that touches each tip of the horns and extends down to the horizon. This spot on the horizon will be roughly south in the northern hemisphere. This trick works when the moon is in any phase except the full moon.

- In the northern hemisphere, water tends to run south, though that southerly flow may be interrupted by topography. But this is true: Water runs downhill, and if you follow it you will eventually reach the confluence of the stream or river and another body of water.

- Check which way low clouds are moving, which is usually different from the wind you feel on your face. Clouds can act as a mirror, much in the way the moon does, and reveal the approximate direction of the sun. If you are lucky you can find clouds in more than one direction that are lit on one side, pinpointing the sun fairly accurately, even if you cannot see it.

- You can estimate how long until the sun sets using your fingers. Extend your arm fully and count the number of finger widths between the sun and the horizon. Each finger is equal to about 15 minutes, which means that four fingers is one hour. This is just an estimate, so allow yourself more time than you measure if you want to get back home before dark.

IN EVERY LANDSCAPE, THE POINT
OF ASTONISHMENT IS THE MEETING
OF THE SKY AND THE EARTH.
—RALPH WALDO EMERSON

NAVIGATION WITHOUT A COMPASS

- To follow up on the previous section, remember there are easy ways to navigate without a compass.

- Use the sun and stars to find north.

- Use trail blazes and markers (see next section).

- Learn to read topographical maps and find your position by comparing the physical landscape and landmarks with the details on the map.

  - Use big landmarks to track your location.

  - Follow the edges of a body of water.

  - Learn to walk a straight line in a forest. All you have to do is line up three objects in a straight line, with you at the center, then walk to the next object and that becomes the new center. For example, Tree A, you and Rock B, and Tree C are all in a straight line. Walk to Tree C and look back at Rock B. Tree C now becomes position B and you choose a new point C ahead that is in line with the previous two points. Using this method, you can bypass optical illusions coming from curves in the land. You also have landmarks to use to retrace your steps.

- Use the general awareness method. Stay alert and use your senses: Stop often and look around you, examine each of the four directions and closely look at the features of the landscape, notice when you are going uphill or downhill, see if you can point to the trail, and try to point toward the last place you stopped.

- Draw your own maps to truly develop your mapping skills.

- Take the lost test. With a partner, head out into an area that is new to you, but which has definite boundaries, like a forest in between a creek with trails on all sides. Simulate a lost scenario in this controlled setting with you heading out and your partner watching from the starting point, keeping track of you from a distance. Make sure you set up a system to contact your partner in case they lose track of you, or if you become truly lost and cannot find your way back.

- Most people get lost because they get scared. Fear and adrenaline can dull your senses, and you may make quick decisions with unwanted consequences. Be prepared for this to happen if you get a bit turned around in a forest. Stay calm, even though you are uncomfortable. Stop, relax, and look around. Identify landmarks and distinctive vegetation. Identify the four directions.

- Use these questions to recover from being lost: What do you know about this landscape? What landmarks are nearby? What is the overall slope and shape of the forest? Where is the nearest water? How does the trail system work here? What trees or plant patterns were next to the trail before you walked off it? What can you hear (like highway noise)?

- If you suspect the trail is south of you, try walking 10 paces and see if you notice anything familiar. If it does not seem right, go back the 10 paces to where you started and try 10 paces in a different direction.

- Gradually expand your search in concentric circles outward. It is only a matter of time until you spot something you recognize, or the trail itself.

- Remember the sun rises in the east and sets in the west.

- Train in navigation skills by finding an area where you can practice all these different skills.

FOLLOWING A TRAIL'S BLAZES AND MARKERS

- If the trail you want to hike is obvious and well marked, you can usually follow it by sight without having to refer to a compass, map, or GPS.

- If the outline of a trail becomes harder to see, if you are uncertain you are headed in the right direction, or if you've lost track of how far you've hiked—those are times when you can refer to navigation aids. But most of the time, it is faster and simpler to follow a trail without any instruments, so you need to know what to look for.

- The best place to learn these skills is by hiking, building up from well-marked trails to more obscure ones that require careful observation skills.

- Hiking trails are carefully planned, built, and maintained using a standard set of construction, signage, and trail marking conventions that are designed to make trails easy to follow.

- All trails have a beginning and an end. The start of a trail is usually signed with the name of the trail or sometimes a number to identify it.

- The point where a trail starts is called the trailhead and often has parking spaces nearby or pullouts where you can leave a vehicle. Many trailheads have an information kiosk with a map, information about the organization that built and maintains the trail, regulations, and safety notices. Take a photo of the map before you head out. When parking at a trailhead in a neighborhood, respect residents and don't block driveways.

- The surface of a trail that you walk on is called the tread. It is usually made with native soil, gravel, or stone that has been compacted to create a hard but natural-looking surface.

FUN FACT

In the 1920s, Vermont's Long Trail became the nation's first long-distance trail, with 273 miles in place.

- Logs backed by shallow trenches (water bars) may be angled across the tread to help direct water off the trail. A wet area may have stepping-stones or bog bridges. Fallen logs may be left along the sides of a trail to mark the boundaries. At higher elevations, there may be low stone (scree) walls to keep hikers on the trail.

- Trails are usually 4 to 6 feet wide and cleared of intruding vegetation, which is periodically cut back by trail workers. If a trail crosses a grass-covered area, you will likely see a bare earthen path in the grass. If a trail runs through a wooded area, it may be littered by dry leaves and forest duff.

- Blazes are 2- to 6-inch colored rectangles painted on trees alongside a trail to mark it at points where the tread becomes hard to see or follow. The same color is used all along that trail. Any intersecting trails will use different-colored blazes. Some trail systems use metal discs or other markers instead of rectangular blazes.

- Blazes are placed along a trail in both directions of travel. If you are following a blazed trail and have not seen a blaze in a while, turn around. You might see a blaze going back in the opposite direction. It will confirm that you are still on track.

- Blazes may be grouped to form patterns. Sometimes for turns that are easy to miss, there are two staggered blazes indicating an upcoming left or right turn.

- One blaze above two: start of trail. One blaze: continue straight. Two blazes one above the other: caution. Two blazes one above the other with a third to the right: spur leading to different trail. Two blazes above one: end of trail.

FOR ME AN ADVENTURE IS SOMETHING THAT I CAN TAKE AN ACTIVE PART IN BUT THAT I DON'T HAVE TOTAL CONTROL OVER.
—PETER CROFT

- Rock cairns (large conical rock piles) may also be used to mark trails, often above the timberline where trees and shrubs do not grow.

  - Trail junctions are usually signed and can be used to confirm that you are hiking your intended trail. Trail junction signs usually have a "You Are Here" indication, mileage, and arrows pointing to the continuation of the trail.

  - Trails that climb hills are often built using switchbacks, where the tread is angled up a hill to the right before turning hard left to climb the next part. Hikers need to pay close attention on a zigzag hill trail. Do not "cut" switchbacks.

- Redundancy is never wasted. Take a map (or two) with you. Have a GPS or a phone with a trail app and GPS.

NAVIGATION WITH GPS OR TRAIL APPS

- GPS is in everything now, from your car to your phone to your dog's collar. But a dedicated handheld GPS receiver is still a valuable tool for many hikers.

- Innovation in phone technology mimics traditional GPS handhelds. A dedicated GPS has the advantages of being much more rugged and water-resistant than a phone, with field-replaceable batteries, superior satellite reception in remote areas, and other special features.

- A GPS receiver does not replace your map and compass. Finding your way out of the backcountry should not be entrusted to just battery-operated electronics.

- A simple GPS unit has a wide range of settings and features. To buy the best unit for your needs, consult retail experts like REI and L.L.Bean. And when you buy a unit, read the owner's manual and practice in your neighborhood or a park until you are comfortable with how everything works. There are GPS navigation courses online and in outdoor gear stores.

- All GPS receivers display your position in coordinates and show your position on a base or topo map.

- Tracking can be turned on so that your tracks are recorded automatically, laying down digital "bread crumbs" called track points at regular intervals. These can be used to retrace your steps or uploaded to a computer and evaluated later.

  - A GPS can give you the direction and distance to a location or waypoint, navigating you point to point. The waypoints can be entered before you head out. In the field, you can mark a waypoint you would like to return to, such as the trailhead or your campsite.

  - A GPS has an odometer/altimeter-like function that tells you how far and how high you have hiked.

FUN FACT

Frederick Law Olmsted's "Keep off the grass" signs in Central Park were intended to allow the carefully designed landscape to be revealed to walkers in an orderly manner that maximized the experience and presumably would encourage them to take additional walks.

- Get a reliable hiking guide and read the entire hike description, as well as turn-by-turn directions before you hit the trail. Take note of trailhead GPS coordinates, and compare the map on your GPS with the trail map in the book.

- Develop a GPS routine for the start of every hike: Acquire satellites, reset trip data, clear track log, set a waypoint at the trailhead, calibrate compass, and calibrate barometer/altimeter.

- GPS units use lithium batteries and have a recharging feature, which is great for day hikes. Make sure you put in fresh batteries before a long trip and always carry spares. Protect spare batteries by putting them in a plastic bag; store them in your first-aid kit. Learn tricks for extending battery life, too, like using battery-saver mode, turning off Bluetooth, turning on airplane mode, lowering screen brightness, etc.

  - A trail app can be used to find your next hiking trail, plot a route, or scout out options for camping along the way. These apps have easy-to-read modern topo maps, as well as historical or classic maps. You can download off-line maps, record your hikes, and get map overlays including contour lines, slope angles, and hill shading.

- Trails on an app can be sorted by activity, suitability/accessibility, and popularity. You can search by trail length, difficulty, elevation gain, route type, and amount of trail traffic. You can read other hikers' reviews and see photos of the route. You can also see weather forecasts and layers that show private land, public land, and wildfire activity.

- With a trail app, while in range of a data signal, you can go to the trail details screen of your desired trail, where you can keep track of your progress and also record it. Turn off your phone's automatic locking feature so that you can always see where you are on the trail.

- You can also download trail maps to your phone or GPS device. The map and your current location are recorded in your device/phone. Use the app's "record" feature, and the trail map you loaded will show your progress and mark what you have traveled.

- Most GPS trail apps work whether you have cell (cellular network) service or not because they work off satellites. If you get really lost, some (like AllTrails) have a feature that sends a status update to your designated safety contact with your location after a certain amount of time.

- A general map source like Google Maps can be used to plan treks, calculate elevation gain and loss, and navigate to trailheads. You can see 2D or 3D maps, explore distances, and zoom in on trail features like slope angles and water sources.

STAND STILL. THE TREES AHEAD AND BUSH BESIDE YOU ARE NOT LOST.
—ALBERT EINSTEIN

USING A TOPO MAP

- Learning to read a topo (topographic) map is essential, as it gives rich detail of the terrain you will be hiking. Simple trail maps are useful for planning but not for navigation in the field. Topo maps show contours, elevations, land features, bodies of water, and vegetation.

- A map and compass is your best backup to a navigation system such as GPS, and you will gain an invaluable understanding of the ground you are hiking.

- Topographic maps help you visualize 3D terrain from a flat piece of paper through contour lines that indicate the steepness of the terrain. Contour lines connect points that share the same elevation.

- To get a topo map, go to the USGS National Geospatial Program US Topo Maps for America website, which has continually updated map data. You can download and print maps from there, but there are some drawbacks to this method.

- There are also companies (DeLorme, National Geographic) that make enhanced topo maps for popular areas. These often include highlighted trails, elevation callouts, distances between trail junctions and landmarks, and more. A good hiking guide will direct you to the best current, accurate topographical map resource for each hike.

- Many apps and websites offer hikers the option of customizing and downloading maps.

- National parks and forests, state parks, and recreational areas usually produce maps, which can be found on their websites. They offer printed and/or downloadable topo maps.

FUN FACT

Seventy-nine percent of the national parks in the United States are located west of the Mississippi River.

- The map's scale tells you how detailed it is. A 1:24,000 scale means 1 inch equals 24,000 inches (2,000 feet) of actual area on the ground. There is a representative scale on the map that helps you visualize actual distance. You can use the scale and a string or the edge of a compass to roughly estimate hiking distance on your map.

- Learn the map legend and what each line, symbol, and color means. Maps also include scale, contour- and index-line intervals, grid systems, and magnetic declination (needed to set up a compass). Ground distances on maps are usually given in feet or miles.

- Different colors on the map show the nature of the vegetation—darker colors mean denser vegetation, lighter means thin vegetation or open terrain. Bodies of water are usually blue.

- Where contour lines are close together, the elevation is changing rapidly in a short distance and the terrain is steep. Where contour lines are wide apart, the elevation is changing slowly, indicating a gentle slope.

- Contour lines also indicate the shape of the terrain. Roughly concentric circles show peaks, for example. A circle with tick marks inside it indicates a depression rather than a peak.

- Every fifth contour line is a thicker index line. At some point along that line, its exact elevation is listed.

- Each map has a set contour interval (found in the map legend) of 40 feet or 80 feet. An 80-foot interval means that each contour line is 80 vertical feet away from the next closest line.

FUN FACT

In 1876, a group in Boston started the Appalachian Mountain Club, which was the first permanently organized hiking club in the United States. There were 108 men and women in the original club. Its predecessors were the Alpine Club of Williamstown, Massachusetts (1863), and the White Mountain Club of Portland, Maine (1873).

- Practice reading features from a map of a familiar area. You can visualize how the terrain of major landmarks relates to the contour lines on the map.

- When you get to the trailhead, orient the map correctly (see the next section on using a compass) and mentally note landmarks during your hike. As you more regularly use topo maps, you will reinforce your ability to know exactly where you are.

- Use a smartphone and GPS as tools to learn. When hiking with a topo map and compass, check your calculations against your device. Does your supposed location on the topo map match the blue dot on your phone? You should never rely solely on battery-operated, satellite-dependent technology to navigate without a backup.

USING A COMPASS

- You should not rely exclusively on a phone or GPS receiver because batteries can die and gadgets can malfunction or get damaged. A magnetized compass and paper topographical map and the knowledge to use them are part of the Ten Essentials. The best way to learn is by taking a course with an outdoor organization or an online class that includes practice outdoors.

- There are many different kinds of compasses, but the most common is the baseplate compass, which has a liquid-filled compass face attached to a flat piece of plastic. Lensatic compasses flip open and use a sighting wire in the cover and a rear lens to take highly accurate bearings. However, lensatic compasses are harder to learn. The following information refers to baseplate compasses because they are the most widely used.

- Get to know the parts of your compass: baseplate, ruler, direction-of-travel arrow, and rotating bezel. The needle housing has an index line, magnetized needle, orienting arrow, and orienting lines.

- Adjust declination first. Magnetic north (where the compass needle points) and true north differ by a few degrees, which is called declination. To adjust for it, you have to find the declination value where you are hiking. Though topo maps list it, it varies over time. Read your compass's instructions for how to adjust for declination.

- Once your compass's declination is set, you do not have to change it until you travel to a faraway place. Once it is set, move on to orienting your map.

- Orient the map by placing the compass on the map with the direction-of-travel arrow pointing toward the top of the map (north). Rotate the bezel so that N is lined up with the direction-of-travel arrow. Slide the baseplate until one of its straight edges aligns with either the left or right edge of the map. The direction-of-travel arrow should still be pointing toward the top of the map.

- Holding the map and compass steady, rotate your body until the end of the magnetic needle is within the outline of the orienting arrow. Done!

- Once you have the map oriented correctly, you can identify nearby landmarks on it. Become familiar with the map before heading off on the hike and keep checking the map along the way.

- Taking a bearing is a navigationally precise way to describe a direction; for example, instead of heading northwest, you follow a bearing of 315 degrees. You can use a bearing to get to a location any time you know where you are on a map.

- To take a bearing, set the compass on the map so the straight side of the baseplate lines up between your current position and the destination. Make sure the direction-of-travel arrow is pointing in the general direction of the destination.

- Rotate the bezel until the orienting lines on the compass are aligned with the north–south grid lines and/or the left and right edges of the map. The north marker on the bezel should point north on the map. Look at the index line to read the bearing.

- Once you have the bearing, hold the compass with the direction-of-travel arrow pointing away from you. Rotate your body until the magnetized needle is inside the orienting arrow. The direction-of-travel arrow is now facing the bearing, and you can follow it to your destination.

- A bearing can also be used to find where you are on a map when you want to know where you are on a trail.

- Find a landmark that you can also identify on your map. Hold the compass flat with the direction-of-travel arrow pointing away from you and at the landmark. Rotate the bezel until the magnetized needle is inside the orienting arrow. Look at the index line to read the bearing.

- Transfer that bearing to your map to find your location. Lay the compass on the map and align one corner of the straight edge with the landmark. The direction-of-travel arrow should also be pointed toward the landmark.

- Rotate the entire baseplate until the orienting lines are running north–south and the north marker on the bezel points to north on the map. You can then draw a line on the map along the straight edge of the compass. The point where the line from the landmark crosses the trail is your location.

- Triangulation is a way you can use multiple bearings to find where you are on a map, for times when you are not on a trail. Repeat the steps above to find the bearings of a second and third landmark, preferably at least 60 degrees from the first landmark. If the lines you draw meet at a single point, that is your location. Most of the time, though, the three lines will form a small triangle and your location is within that. A large triangle means you made an error and need to start over.

FUN FACT

Hiking clubs in the United States were first formed in the 1850s.

USING AN ALTIMETER

- An altimeter is a device that determines your altitude/ elevation above sea level. Learning to use and carrying an altimeter is a smart fallback for navigation.

- Backpacking has become more high-tech over the past few decades. Hikers now have multiple GPS-enabled devices such as a smartphone, watch, and two-way messenger that duplicate altimeter, barometer, and compass functions to pinpoint location, navigate to waypoints, and track route, speed, distance, altitude, and vertical change.

- You want to create the lightest, least expensive, and most electrically efficient navigation system possible that quickly delivers the information you need and want.

  - If you are on a trail with ascents and descents covered by forest canopy or lacking major landmarks, an altimeter can be used in conjunction with a map and compass to pinpoint your location.

- If you know your altitude, you can double-check landmarks, traverse a contour line without changing elevation, rule out false summits and passes, and confirm your location on a map by cross-referencing your current altitude with nearby topographic features.

- There are stand-alone altimeter/barometer devices, as well as altimeter watches. Some watches (Apple Watch) now have a barometric altimeter so you can track your relative elevation.

- The features that matter most in an altimeter watch are a comfortable fit, the ability to quickly and easily adjust the elevation, and the ability to record and display cumulative elevation gain and loss over the course of a hike.

- An altimeter watch should have a display that shows the elevation numbers prominently. It should have a clock, too, and large buttons that work with gloves or cold hands.

- A barometric altimeter, when used with a topographic map, is more reliable and often more accurate than a GPS receiver for measuring altitude. A GPS signal may be unavailable or it may give inaccurate altitudes when all available satellites are near the horizon.

- Altimeter watches rely on barometric pressure to calculate altitude. As barometric pressure fluctuates, so does the altitude reading. Be aware this can cause serious errors.

- It is important to recalibrate the altimeter regularly by resetting it to the correct reading when a known altitude is reached. Read the elevation from a map and adjust the altimeter accordingly. This is important in mountainous areas where the pressure may change rapidly as weather systems come in.

- Knowing how high you are and how far you still have to climb is a great way of monitoring your progress on an ascent or descent. This is particularly helpful when there is low visibility or few landmarks.

- Checking your ascent rate is a way of monitoring progress. By checking your increasing altitude and the time taken, you can estimate your arrival time at a given spot, like a summit.

- If you are descending or ascending, you can use an altimeter and map if you need to make a change of direction (e.g., to avoid steep and craggy ground).

- Use an altimeter to follow a contour line and maintain the same height as you traverse around a slope in low visibility. Check that the altitude reading remains constant as you traverse.

- You can learn how to predict weather in the mountains with an altimeter and barometer.

- Now that GPS technology is ubiquitous, the best devices for backpackers in the mountains include GPS watch, smartphone with GPS app, handheld GPS unit, and/or satellite messenger.

UNMARKED/OFF-TRAIL NAVIGATION

- Off-trail navigation is for the experienced hiker/ backpacker. If you are bushwhacking, dress appropriately, keep your compass attached to your body, and carry two copies of your map(s) protected in a ziplock bag.

- Bring a couple of pencils to mark the map. Draw grid lines on the map before the hike to make it easier to take accurate bearings in the field.

- If you are going off-trail or navigating unmarked backcountry, you need to be completely competent at using a map and compass, and you must have survival skills. You also need a GPS and a personal locator beacon (PLB).

- Your map should cover all the territory you plan to be in. Try to sketch out a route. If you are simply exploring the area, it is not as crucial, but long point-to-point journeys require preparation. You may need additional, more detailed maps for certain areas. Once you have the right maps, you can augment them with a GPS unit.

- GPS units work best when you download topographic maps. You can then use landmarks on the GPS, match them to your map, and figure out your location.

- GPS waypoints and track logs are two key features to use. Waypoints are precise locations you can mark on the GPS unit. Track logs record your exact route, drawing a line on the GPS screen showing where you have been. This is ideal for retracing your tracks.

- The goal is to find the overall path of least resistance between two points.

- To do that you must take into account the effects of horizontal distance, vertical change, vegetation, ground cover, game trails, and time sinks (e.g., blowdowns, brush thickets, canyons, cliffs and ledges, deep water, loose moraine slopes).

- The best line of travel rarely cuts against the grain of the landscape. It usually runs directly with or against the natural downhill course between two points (fall lines) and takes advantage of any weakness in the landscape. If you are in a thick patch of trees blocking you from the other side of a creek, the best line of travel is to penetrate the patch where it is thinnest.

- Simplify your route by using natural features.

- Follow a creek, ridgeline, or shoreline.

- Hike until you run into a creek, ridgeline, or trail.

- Hike along natural hazards like creek fords and snowfields.

- Develop your powers of observation. Notice which way the streams run, where the lakes are, and if any hills or mountains rise above the surrounding landscape. Notice gaps or passes between ranges.

- Keep an eye out for areas devoid of vegetation, such as bogs, meadows, or open summits.

- Turn around and observe how landmarks appear when you approach them from another direction.

- Make it a habit to constantly check your map and know your position, looking around to verify it by terrain-to-map association, altimeter, or visible landmarks. It takes a lot of experience to become good at off-trail navigation.

NAVIGATING WATER

- Crossing creeks, rivers, or streams can seem intimidating, but learning some skills will make crossing safe and fairly enjoyable. Always exercise caution when in and around water sources.

- To assess how deep and fast the water is, throw a rock into the water and listen for the "plop." If you can see the bottom, did the rock disappear quickly downstream? If you can't see the bottom because it is muddy or milky, throw a stick and see how far it travels downstream in 10 seconds. Listen for the sound of rocks rolling in the water. Scout out what is on the far bank, where you will try to emerge.

- Trekking poles are extremely helpful when navigating water. They allow you to have three points of contact in the water at all times. The poles are also great for probing the water and testing the current. If you feel resistance against your pole, it's likely your legs will feel it even more.

- Hiking boots/shoes become even more important in water. You need tread on wet surfaces and protection against objects hiding under the water's surface.

- Always unbuckle the waist strap of your backpack before approaching a water source. That way, if you fall into the water your pack won't weigh you down.

- Cross the calmest section of current, even if that means hiking up- or downstream (if possible, avoid walking in the stream or river) to find the best crossing.

- It can be easier to walk on the rocks along the edge of a stream or river than in the vegetation running alongside it. Check the condition of logs, rocks, and other materials near water.

- Test the stability of logs or rocks as you move. Use trekking poles, a hiking stick, or even a single foot to help determine if your next step will be stable. Rocks with craggier surfaces may be less slick than flat rocks.

- Avoid water that is higher than your knees. Deep water can make you lose your balance or sweep you off your feet.

- When crossing, face upstream to pinpoint where faster currents are flowing.

- Always wear footwear when crossing. Carry water shoes or other fast-drying shoes on trips where you know there are water crossings. Many hikers use lightweight trail running shoes or waterproof camp shoes. They need to be stable on your feet and protective.

- Never cross above a waterfall or a logjam.

- If you are hiking with others, crossing a body of water as a group is a safer way to navigate stronger currents. Having one hiker follow the leader allows them to benefit from blocked current and help stabilize the leader. You can form a triangle with two others for extra stability.

- Rivers have various layers of water moving at different speeds. The lower layer moves more slowly than the top layer. The layers next to the bottom and sides are slowest. The top layer is the only one affected by air.

- While your feet can have good traction on the river bottom, your knees will take the force of the current, which could knock you over. Reading the speed, depth, and flow of the water will help you determine if it is safe to cross.

- If it does not seem safe to cross a body of water, do not risk it. It is better to turn back.

SAFETY AND HEALTH

HIKING IS A BIT LIKE LIFE: THE JOURNEY ONLY
REQUIRES YOU TO PUT ONE FOOT IN FRONT OF
THE OTHER . . . AGAIN AND AGAIN AND AGAIN.
AND IF YOU ALLOW YOURSELF OPPORTUNITY
TO BE PRESENT THROUGHOUT THE ENTIRETY OF
THE TREK, YOU WILL WITNESS BEAUTY EVERY
STEP OF THE WAY, NOT JUST AT THE SUMMIT.
—UNKNOWN

THERE'S NOTHING QUITE LIKE IMMERSING YOURSELF IN the great outdoors by hiking. There's fresh air, peace and quiet, and amazing nature all around. But there are real risks to your safety and health, too. You are in nature's home, not yours, and unexpected things can and do happen in the wilderness.

You can minimize your odds of encountering an emergency while hiking and equip yourself to handle one if it comes up. The "Preparation and Planning" chapter earlier in this book set you up nicely; in this chapter, you'll learn some specifics to make you even more ready.

FUN FACT

Hiking the Appalachian Trail usually takes between five and seven months, and only one in four who attempt the thru-hike are successful.

BEGINNER HIKING MISTAKES

- Not bringing the Ten Essentials.

- Forgetting something important, like insect repellent, sunscreen, a snack, water, or GPS. You need the Ten Essentials.

- Not eating and drinking enough before or during the hike.

- Bringing too much gear. Bringing cans or store-packaged food.

- Not using or carrying a map on a familiar route.

- Not considering the weather.

- Not considering time and pace.

- Not learning basic navigation and practicing those skills.

- Overconfidence. Hiking too far or too fast too soon. Trying to do too much.

- Not finding the right footwear.

- Not properly using trekking poles.

- Not wearing the right clothing. Not wearing layers. Wearing cotton.

- Not being familiar with your daypack/backpack or packing it improperly.

- Not following Leave No Trace principles.

- Ignoring storm signs.

- Getting caught in the dark.

- Not hiking your own hike. Hike when and how you want for your body type and temperament. Don't allow others to negatively influence your hike.

TRAILHEAD SECURITY

- Choose either a popular hiking spot or a very remote hiking spot. The riskiest trailheads are the ones that receive moderate use (around six cars) and those that are on or close to a main road. Trailheads with many people coming and going are safer. Trailheads that are difficult to reach are fairly safe.

- Check with the ranger or public lands manager about any crime incidents at the trailhead.

- If hiking in an urban park, complete your hike before dark.

- Make sure your automotive insurance covers theft and vandalism.

- If you have an older, dirtier vehicle to use, opt for that. You might also consider a drop-off or shuttle service.

- Remove any bumper sticker or sign that shows an opinion or support for something that may be unpopular in the area you are hiking.

- Look around the trailhead parking lot for any evidence of previous break-ins—like broken automobile glass on the ground.

- Be aware of other people at the trailhead. You don't want to exercise an unconscious bias, but you must look out for your personal safety. If people are not dressed for hiking or if you are uncomfortable at the trailhead for any reason, listen to your instincts and go somewhere else.

- Park your vehicle near other vehicles. A higher level of human traffic can deter thieves.

- Do not leave possessions visible in your vehicle.

- If your car is completely empty of possessions, you could choose to leave it unlocked so that thieves can quickly find out there is nothing to steal.

- Leave your wallet or purse at home. Carry the cash you need and any credit or bank cards in your pack or on your person. Take any small, expensive gear such as a camera with you.

- Never leave money in plain view in a car.

- If you don't have one already, install a car alarm. Display stickers that show you have a car alarm.

- Never trust your trunk as a safe storage area for anything.

- Consider using an antitheft device if your vehicle model is one that is stolen frequently.

- Report any theft you do suffer immediately.

YOU CAN'T BE SUSPICIOUS OF A TREE, OR
ACCUSE A BIRD OR SQUIRREL OF SUBVERSION
OR CHALLENGE THE IDEOLOGY OF A VIOLET.
—HAL BORLAND

WHEN NOT TO HIKE

- When it is forbidden in an area due to a crisis, like a pandemic.
- In the middle of a storm or if the weather is so severe that visibility and your ability to find your way would be compromised.
- When a storm is forecast, especially one involving precipitation and high wind.
- In high winds with gusts forecast.
- When you are injured, especially with a leg injury.
- If the trail immediately looks to be beyond your capabilities.
- When you are not prepared to take your time and hike safely.
- When you are uncomfortable continuing the hike and/or are simply no longer enjoying yourself.
- If you forgot the Ten Essentials.
- When there is a park alert, wildfire, trail closure, or other hazard.
- If you start to experience altitude sickness.
- When you run out of water and there are no water sources.
- If you get injured, bit by a snake, or experience a heat-related illness.
- When the bugs are overwhelming and you are not enjoying the hike.
- If there is water you simply cannot cross safely and the only option is to turn back.

- When there is threatening wildlife, like a bear.
- If you have hiked to a point where you are afraid of the height or the exposure (narrow trail with precipitous drops). Or anytime your hike is well beyond your comfort level.
- When daylight is running out and you don't have the proper gear (clothing, shelter) to be stranded for more than a couple of hours.

AVOIDING INJURY

- The most common hiking injuries are blisters, sprains, cuts, hypothermia, hyperthermia, dehydration, sunburn, and bug bites. You can take steps to prevent each of these.

- Prevent injuries by slowing down while navigating difficult terrain, using trekking poles or hands for added balance, testing handholds and footholds before committing your full body weight, tying the laces on your footwear tightly and evenly, keeping your backpack snug against your body, tying down dangling gear, making sure you can climb down anything that you climb up, and staying adequately hydrated.

- To prevent blisters from forming, ensure that your socks do not slip up and down while you walk. Your hiking footwear should fit tightly (but not too tightly) to prevent your foot from moving around or rubbing against the inside. Your footwear should be broken in before a hike. Keeping your feet dry is also important in preventing blisters. Carry one to three spare pairs of socks so you can change them if they get wet.

- The most common type of sprain to occur while hiking is an ankle sprain. Prevention can be as simple as wearing good (broken-in) hiking boots with sturdy ankle support. Only wear trail runners if the trail permits this safely without unduly raising the risk of sprains.

- Take care and caution with foot placement on uneven ground. Trekking poles are a great option because of the extra stability they offer.

- Be careful when passing undergrowth on narrow parts of the trail to prevent cuts and scratches from branches or brambles.

- Hypothermia is the cooling of your core body temperature. Prevent it by making smart gear and layering choices. It is mainly about keeping dry and warm. (See the "First-Aid Instructions" section.)

FUN FACT

The Triple Crown of thru-hiking is the Pacific Crest Trail, the Continental Divide Trail, and the Appalachian Trail—a total of nearly 8,000 miles across twenty-two states with 1 million feet of cumulative elevation gain. Unofficially, it is estimated that only about 600 people have hiked the Triple Crown.

- Hyperthermia is the increase of body temperature when hiking in hot and humid conditions. Prevent it by drinking plenty of fluids, wearing a hat, and using sunscreen.

- The trick to preventing dehydration is drinking plenty of water.

- Use a sunblock of at least 25 SPF and carry it in your pack. A sun hat or cap is also needed on warm, sunny hikes—though you can also get sunburned on cloudy, overcast days.

- Bug bites are difficult to prevent, especially when there are large swarms. Research EPA-registered insect repellents and get one that is recommended and with which you are comfortable (DEET, picaridin, IR3535, oil of lemon eucalyptus, para-menthane-diol, 2-undecanone). Different repellents suit different regions and their accompanying insect types. Check the EPA's "Find the Repellent That Is Right for You" website. And protect other items from insect repellent by storing it in its own ziplock bag.

- A bug headnet is helpful in places where you know there will be swarms. You can also buy a bug jacket, bug pants, and/or bug mittens.

- Clothing treated with EPA-registered permethrin provides odorless wearable protection against ticks, mosquitoes, chiggers, biting flies, ants, and spiders. Protection will fade after a certain amount of washes—spray-on permethrin is available to extend protection.

FUN FACT

The North Country Trail is the longest in the National Trails System, stretching 4,600 miles over seven states from North Dakota to New York.

- Although it is difficult to spot ticks on dark-colored clothing, darker shades tend to attract fewer ticks. Always tuck in your shirt to your pants, and pants into socks. Treat clothing and gear with products containing 0.5 percent permethrin, which will remain protective through several washings.

- Know where to expect ticks and avoid those areas or be prepared with proper clothing and insect repellent. Walk in the center of trails and avoid wooded and brushy areas with high grass and leaf litter.

- After you come indoors, check your clothing for ticks. Take off clothing outside if possible. Tumble-dry clothes on high heat for 10 minutes to kill ticks, or wash in hot water and then dry on hot. Also examine pets, coats, and daypacks. Shower within 2 hours of coming indoors and do a full-body tick check with a handheld or full-length mirror, checking especially under the arms, in and around the ears, inside the belly button, back of the knees, in and around hair, between the legs, and around the waist.

- Beware of hunters. Know the dates of the hunting seasons for where you are hiking. Wear bright colors, particularly blaze orange. Or simply stay off trails and out of the woods during hunting season to avoid risking injury or your life.

TAKING BREAKS

- Your body and mind get tired. Sometimes pain and soreness happen right at the beginning of a hike. Sometimes you poop out with a half mile to go. You need to learn the art of taking breaks. Read the hike description in your guidebook ahead of time and plan breaks at safe resting points.

- Hiking solo is great because you can go at your own pace. With a partner or group, you need to remember that everyone goes at different speeds. Yet, just like when hiking solo, you need to find a pace you are comfortable with.

- A good hiking pace is one that can be maintained for at least an hour without stopping. If you find yourself resting every 30 minutes, try hiking more slowly.

- When your body is telling you to take a rest, you need to listen. When your mind is telling you to take a rest, you need to listen. Look for a good place to rest. Step off the trail where possible without trampling vegetation too much, or at least try to get out of the way of other hikers.

- When you feel like you absolutely can't go on much longer, you need to listen to your instinct. Pushing yourself too hard is how you get injured, ill, or give up on hiking altogether.

- If you are with a group and know you will need frequent breaks, it is best to arrange that before setting off. And it will always help to hike with people who are around the same hiking level as you.

FUN FACT
The National Park System has 18,000 miles of trails.

FUN FACT

The Great Trail (Trans Canada Trail) runs east–west across Canada and is 14,996 miles—the longest recreational multiuse trail network in the world.

- A break is not sitting or lying down and taking a nap, which would make it difficult to get up and continue. It is best to walk around slowly or at least stand until you feel more settled.

- Aim for 5- to 10-minute breaks.

- The ability to sip constantly from a hydration bladder is much easier and more efficient than stopping to pull out a water bottle. With a hydration bladder (or an accessible, holstered bottle), you will stay better hydrated and won't have to stop for water breaks.

- Often a break is needed not because you feel physically tired but because you are hungry. Along with constantly hydrating as you hike, you need to ingest snacks that are nutritious, give you energy, and aren't heavy/too filling. On your breaks, eat and drink water.

- If you are not stopping to relieve yourself every so often, you may not be drinking enough water.

- With a little practice and a slightly slower pace, anyone can eat while they hike. Doing this may provide a more balanced energy intake. Lunch foods can be divided into smaller-sized portions and treated similarly to snacks.

- Before you resume the hike after a break, do some stretches. Stretching keeps blood flowing, muscles moving, and helps prevent injury. Stretching whenever you take a break can keep you strong.

OUTSIDE LIES MAGIC.
—JOHN STILGOE

- Sometimes changing up a few small things while you hike can affect how many breaks you need to take. Getting into hiking condition is always advised. Practicing smaller hikes, wearing supportive shoes, and using trekking poles can help with comfort and endurance.

- You may also need breaks for retrieving or switching out gear. Try to prevent too much of this by keeping items you need readily accessible. Apply sunscreen before you leave. Have your map handy and check it frequently. Make sure you have the right layers on.

- Pee breaks should be quick enough to not require a group break. Don't wait for the person peeing; just keep hiking at a slower pace until they catch up. Make sure your partner knows this, but be sure to stop at any junctions so you don't lose your partner.

- On longer hikes, there are mandatory breaks: reaching a summit or a hiking viewpoint, refilling water, a pooping bathroom break, blister prevention, applying first aid, and completing a ford of a body of water.

GOING TO THE BATHROOM IN THE WOODS

- New hikers need to learn and practice going to the bathroom in the woods. The first step is following Leave No Trace principles. Find out if there are any regulations on human waste in the area you are going; sensitive or heavily traveled areas may require you to pack out solid human waste. Always pack trail hygiene essentials: hand sanitizer, wipes, and sealable quart-size plastic bags.

- Don't wait until the last moment—you will need a few minutes to find the right spot. To pee, choose a place well away from the trail or campsite. Move 200 feet (about 70 steps) away from a water source such as a lake or stream.

- Find a soft spot of earth that absorbs quickly so you won't get splashed (e.g., pine needles). Watch the slope so that the pee runs away from you, and make sure clothes, boot laces, and straps are out of the way. A wide stance keeps you balanced.

- A pee funnel lets you pee standing up. This can be helpful when it is cold, rainy, or in areas with no privacy. It takes practice! Rinse the pee funnel if possible and carry in a plastic bag.

- On a day hike, carry toilet paper or tissue and a small ziplock bag. Put the used paper in the bag and dump the paper in your toilet when you get home.

- A "pee rag" can be used, rinsed (if possible) and tied to the outside of your pack. Campers may employ a pee bottle (with a pee funnel).

- For a poop, you need toilet paper, hand sanitizer, ziplock bag, camp trowel, and— for high-elevation or sensitive areas— solid waste bags/containers.

- Find an appropriate spot for a poop. Take your supplies 200 feet (70 steps) from the trail, water sources, or campsite. Choose underbrush for privacy if you like. Pay attention to the surroundings so you can find your way back to the trail or camp.

- If possible, find loose, rich soil and a sunny site, which help decompose waste more quickly. Use a trowel, stick, rock, or boot heel to make a "cat hole" about 4 inches wide and 6 to 8 inches deep.

- If the ground is hard or rocky, try lifting a partially embedded rock and use that spot. Replace the rock when you are done.

- Use as little toilet paper as possible. You can also use nonpoisonous leaves, smooth stones, or snowballs to wipe off. Put the paper in a waste bag to pack out.

  - Pre-moistened wipes can be nice to use, and also need to be packed out in a waste bag (as do menstrual supplies).

  - Fill the cat hole with the original dirt, tamp it down, and place a rock or branch over or upright on the covered hole to discourage digging critters.

  - Unwashed hands can lead to intestinal ailments during or after your trip.

- Always use hand sanitizer or wipes after you poop (and before handling food). Soap and water is more thorough, if you have that option. On a backpacking trip, you should thoroughly wash your hands at least once a day with soap and water. Dry your hands with a different towel or bandanna than you use for drying dishes.

- Soap should be unscented and biodegradable. Consider carrying a small, fast-drying pack towel.

AVOIDING INSECTS

- Depending on the season, time of day, and weather, your hike may be spectacular or burdened by thousands of obnoxious insects the entire time.

- From late fall to early spring, insects are less of a concern. That is your most comfortable hiking season.

- If you hike in warmer weather, like summer, wear long-sleeved shirts and long pants. Very lightweight, light-colored clothes can be cool enough yet keep most of your skin protected.

- Wearing light-colored clothes makes it easier to see insects while they are still on the outside of your clothes. Some hikers opt for dark-colored clothes because insects and ticks are not as drawn to them. But dark-colored clothes absorb heat from the sun, which is not always optimal.

- Tuck pants into socks. Tuck shirt into pants.

- Wear permethrin-treated clothes or spray it on your clothes yourself. It kills ticks rather than repelling them and lasts through many clothes washings.

- Use DEET-based insect repellents (15 to 30 percent solution) on exposed skin, or the insect repellent of your choice.

- Wear a hat both for sun protection and to keep insects out of your hair. Ticks can drop off birds and out of trees that birds were in.

- Consider an insect headnet, jacket, mittens, or full-body suit if you want to protect yourself even more and don't care what it looks like.

- Avoid brushy areas, hanging branches, and tall grass. Try to walk in the middle of the trail.

- Try to hike on open, sunny trails rather than in shady, protected forest. Sunny, dry areas can still have ticks, but fewer than shady, damp areas.

- Wind will blow mosquitoes away, and drier air is harder on bugs.

- Check each other for ticks as you and your partner hike and when you stop for breaks.

- To avoid mosquitoes, hike during the morning and early afternoon. Be off the trail before sunset.

- Almost all spiders are venomous, but very few have venom powerful enough to bother humans. To prevent a spider bite, never reach bare skin someplace you cannot see, like into holes, around branches, and under rocks (or wear gloves). If you are hiking through trees, move trekking poles or a hiking stick in a circle in front of you to remove spider webs before walking into them. Look before you sit down or lean against a tree to rest.

- To avoid bees, yellow jackets, hornets, and wasps, first remember that they are mainly looking for flowers. Avoid wearing bright or flower-patterned clothes and shiny jewelry. Avoid perfume and scented lotion or deodorant. If a bee or wasp is bothering you, slowly move away down the trail. Swatting or rapid movement can provoke an attack.

- Strongly odorous food can attract insects. Keep your food and garbage sealed. Don't drink from cans—a bug may have gotten inside trying to get to the sweet, sugary liquid. Likewise, look in a cup before you drink from it.

USING INSECTICIDES

- When it comes to preventing mosquito and tick bites, it is important to remain vigilant and stay protected in the outdoors. That includes using insect repellents for your skin and clothing.

- An effective repellent is one of the best ways to keep biting bugs away. *Consumer Reports* offers insect repellent ratings and lists top products offering several hours of protection.

- The Centers for Disease Control and Prevention (CDC) also recommends another strategy on top of repellent: treating your clothing with a pesticide called permethrin. A pesticide kills bugs on contact.

- Permethrin-treated clothing is available from various manufacturers, especially those that specialize in outdoor gear. L.L.Bean will treat your clothes with permethrin for you if you mail them in. Check other companies as well.

- You can spray your own clothes with a permethrin spray.

- Is permethrin-treated clothing a better option for you? Studies are still being done on the two methods. Permethrin spray is only meant for fabric, not for skin, and specifically for outerwear, not underwear.

- DEET-based spray is meant for skin, but can be used on clothing. Avoid spraying DEET on plastics, rayon, spandex, and other synthetic fabrics; DEET can damage those.

- The most important thing to remember when spraying an insecticide or pesticide is to follow the instructions on the label of the product. Either of these types of chemical compounds can cause serious health problems in people exposed to high doses. You don't want permethrin getting directly on your skin, and you don't want to inhale it.

- The dose of permethrin you receive by wearing treated clothing is considered safe, even for pregnant women and children. (It is also in medications for head lice and scabies.)

- Always spray permethrin on clothes while they are off your body. Hang clothes on hangers outside and spray them thoroughly. The clothes should become damp and look a little darker in color.

- Let the clothes dry completely—a few hours, depending on humidity—before you wear them. The clothes you treat yourself need to be retreated often, likely after six washings. A 9-ounce bottle of permethrin will treat one shirt, one pair of pants, and one pair of socks. Clothes and gear that you spray (tent, shoes, backpack) also will need retreating.

- Manufacturers of pre-treated clothing say their products are still effective after many washings (L.L.Bean claims seventy, for example).

- Treated clothing should be washed separately—either by hand-washing or using the gentle cycle of the washing machine. This helps preserve the protection.

- You should only use permethrin approved for clothing, which will be indicated on the product label.

- Do not rely on permethrin alone. Treated clothing is one useful step. But there's always exposed skin vulnerable to bug bites.

  - To protect exposed skin, use an effective insect repellent containing 15 to 30 percent DEET, 20 percent picaridin, or 30 percent oil of lemon eucalyptus.

  - Make sure you apply insect repellent correctly, according to the product label. Put your sunscreen on first, followed by insect repellent.

HIKING ALONE

- Solo hiking can be intimidating. If you get lost or injure yourself, help could be hours or even days away. Female solo hikers may perceive themselves as being more vulnerable than men. But there is a risk for anyone going out in the woods alone.

- While the likelihood of having a problem with another person is slim, all solo hikers should be prepared for every possible scenario.

- Even a basic self-defense course improves your chances of getting away from an attacker.

- Start with solo day hikes and then think about working your way up to staying at an overnight shelter that has a caretaker. Take small steps in building experience as a solo hiker. Don't take unnecessary risks.

- Confidence and self-defense training can improve a lone hiker's chances when faced with an assailant. The more you do the things that make you uncomfortable, the weaker your doubts become.

- Holding yourself with confidence is important. Most attackers are looking for easy prey, someone they can overpower quickly. If you stare them straight in the eye and walk with confidence, you become a less attractive target.

- Never listen to music during a hike. You need to be aware of everything around you.

- Never admit you are alone. Imply you are with other people by saying, "I was scouting ahead for my group," or "I'm waiting for my boyfriend to catch up. He's taking a short break."

- Carry protection. Bear spray works just as well on humans as on bears. Have it readily available and easy to reach. If you have a dog and it is trained to hike, take it with you.

- Act confident and strong. Walk with shoulders back and an open posture if you feel threatened. Make eye contact and say, "What do you want?" or "You need to back off."

- Create distance between you and the threat, whether a person or a mountain lion. The more distance you have, the better chance to avoid a surprise attack. And stay away from roads; the greatest dangers of hiking alone happen near roads.

- Run and fight. Use every trick in the book to escape. Never hesitate to hurt the attacker: Bite, scream, kick, scratch, and punch until you can escape.

- Carry communication devices—a whistle and a reflective LED light with strobe functions. Invest in a personal locator beacon (PLB) or satellite phone (not just a cell phone). Make sure all your devices are fully charged before heading out. And know how you will transmit an emergency signal if necessary (mirror, smoke flare, strobe flasher, smoke signals from a fire).

- Carry a complete first-aid kit and understand how to use it. Know all the contents of your first-aid kit.

- Make sure you check the weather forecast from several resources.

- Gain knowledge about the wildlife and geography of the area you plan to hike in. Learn to identify common animal tracks. If you see an animal carcass, leave the area. Learn what to do if you see a bear. It may not be necessary to carry bear spray everywhere, and it's best to avoid an encounter without being aggressive.

- Leave a note in the car and/or tell a friend which trail you are hiking, what time you are leaving, and when you expect to return. Never transmit your coordinates or whereabouts on social media.

IF YOU GET LOST

- The best tool for survival if you get lost outdoors is advance planning and preparation. You must train for and expect the unexpected and plan accordingly. Even if you are going out for just an hour or a few hours, you should pack the Ten Essentials.

- More often than not, lack of preparation is where problems start. Leading causes of getting lost include improper or no maps, forgetting a compass or GPS, starting out too late in the day, being ill-prepared for bad weather, splitting up a group on the trail, being unprepared for difficult trail conditions, and ignoring obvious signs to turn back.

- Know your route: where you are going and how to return. Plan your trip carefully. Read the entire hike description and miles and directions in your guidebook. Take a picture of the hike map.

- Have more than enough food and water for the activity you plan.

- Take a compass and reliable map and a navigation app that you know how to use. You may want a GPS and cell phone, but know that there might not be a signal and the battery can fail. To attempt to find a signal: Try the highest ground available with an unobstructed view of the sky to improve line-of-sight connection to cell towers, hold the phone at arm's length away from your body and rotate your body to find reception, and keep making calls from the same location (a cell phone remembers where the nearest towers are located). Send a text message to your emergency contact (requires less power than a voice call), or tell an emergency dispatcher about the location—elevation, landmarks, position of sun, terrain, and last known location.

- Wear appropriate footwear and layered clothing, and pack extras in case what you are wearing gets wet. Bring high-quality hiking gear.

- Tell someone the exact details of where you are going, the trail you plan to follow, the vehicle you are driving and where you plan to park, how many people are with you, and when you plan to return.

- Stop. As soon as you realize you may be lost, stop, stay calm, and stay put. Take deep breaths to slow your racing mind. Stay put until you feel calm. Panic is your biggest enemy. Signs you are in trouble: A formerly clear trail dwindles to a barely traveled path, blazes and other markings disappear or change, a trail climbs when it should be descending or vice versa (think back to the topo map you reviewed in advance), the sun is positioned in the wrong part of the sky for the direction you were supposed to be hiking, the middle of the trail is blocked by two sticks or logs crossed like an X, footprints made by other hikers disappear.

- Think. Go over in your mind how you got to where you are. What landmarks should you be able to see? Do not move at all until you have a specific reason to take a step.

- Observe. Get your compass out and determine the directions based on where you are standing. Know which way is north, south, east, and west. Do not walk aimlessly, and if you are on a trail, stay on it. Use the map to try to determine how far you hiked on the trail; some phones and apps will tell you how far you hiked. Try to gauge the distance you have gone using the map. You may be able to retrace your steps.

- Consider turning off your phone if you do not have reception or an off-line compass on it. This will conserve your battery until you are in an area with a signal.

- As a last resort, follow a stream or drainage downhill, which could lead to a trail or road. This must be done with caution.

Plan. Based on your thinking and observations, come up with possible plans. Choose and act on one of them. But if you are not very confident in the plan or route, it is better to stay put. If it is nightfall, you are injured, or you feel near exhaustion—stay in place. Those are basically your two choices: staying put or hiking out.

- By staying put, you make it easier for a search party to find you. You will need to make a shelter and create a rescue signal—a mirror, a whistle, or a smoky controlled fire. If someone flies overhead, put your arms up in a Y position, which indicates "yes," you need to be rescued. (One arm over your head indicates "no," you do not need to be rescued.)

- If you are confident of the path and decide to try to find your way out, stay on the trail to avoid getting more lost. All trails are marked with signs, blazes, or markers.

- If you decide to rescue yourself, follow these guidelines: Stop and rest when you feel tired; rest in the shade for at least 30 minutes when you stop to eat; if you eat and still feel tired, continue to rest.

- Drink enough water to avoid dehydration.

- Fix small problems while they are still small. If you keep pushing and ignore your body, the pain or illness will get worse and make self-rescue more difficult.

- On hot days, avoid hiking between 10 a.m. and 4 p.m. Find a shady spot and stay put until the temperature goes down. Hike slowly.

EMERGENCY SHELTER, FIRE, WATER, AND FOOD

- The average person can survive 3 minutes without air (oxygen) or in icy water. You can survive 3 hours without shelter in a harsh environment. You can survive 3 days without water (if you have shelter). You can survive 3 weeks without food (if you have water and shelter).

- Before heading out on a day hike, ask yourself what other gear, medicine, food, or water you would take if you knew you would not get back before dark or before the next morning.

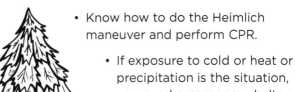

- Put an emergency kit together. If you are outdoors a lot, you may already own many of the necessary supplies.

- If you are in an emergency situation, concentrate on the most immediate problem first. There is no need to think about food if the main threat to your survival is hypothermia because your clothes are wet.

  - Any threat to breathing is an immediate survival situation. Anyone who has asthma or allergic reactions has to be alert and constantly prepared. Such a person should never go anywhere without an inhaler or emergency epinephrine, other prescriptions, and a medical ID.

    - Know how to do the Heimlich maneuver and perform CPR.

      - If exposure to cold or heat or precipitation is the situation, you need emergency shelter. Carry an emergency shelter such as a bivy, and know how to build a shelter using natural materials.

- Know how to make a fire. Pack a firestarter and know how to use it.

- Know the early signs of dehydration: thirst, dry mouth, decrease in energy. The more serious symptoms of dehydration include cramps, headache, nausea, dark urine, stumbling, mumbling, grumbling, and fumbling.

- Know how to find water from a freshwater source or from precipitation that can be collected. Flowing water is a good option; the second-best choice is calm water without a lot of sediment or silt. After a heavy rain, wait before gathering water, as surface material will have washed into it.

- Gather water from the surface of the least murky part of the water source you can find. Strain the water through cloth or use a pre-filter before treating the water. Keep your hands clean, too.

- One minute (3 minutes above 6,500 feet) of boiling (a rolling boil) is the most reliable way of killing bacteria, parasites, and other pathogens. For this option in an emergency, you will need a container, firestarter, and fire-building knowledge.

- The next option is to carry a survival straw—one of the smallest, lightest tools for filtering. Or, there are two types of water filters to use with a hydration bladder: pump-action and drip/suction.

- Water disinfection tablets are popular and effective. They do have an expiration date, so be aware. Different tablets have different treatment speeds, too. Some are iodine-based and others chlorine-based; research which one is the better choice for you.

- There are water treatment methods employing light: UV light devices (instantaneous) and solar water disinfection (uses the sun's energy, but takes days).

- In most survival scenarios, immediate rescue, shelter, and water are the initial priorities. They are more important than food acquisition.

- Know what you should eat before and during a hike. Understand basic nutrition: Carbohydrates and fats provide energy, protein builds and repairs muscles, and fiber keeps digestion moving. Take a course or get a book about foraging in your area to learn what substances in nature can be eaten, how to acquire them, and how to cook them.

THE VERY BASIC CORE OF A MAN'S LIVING SPIRIT IS HIS PASSION FOR ADVENTURE.
—JON KRAKAUER

EMERGENCY SHELTER OPTIONS

- The location of your emergency shelter is important, and you should stop and think before building it. This section assumes you have a 10-by-10-foot tarp or survival blanket (unless you have a bivy) and paracord or rope. Stakes are handy, but sturdy sticks can be used.

- The direction from which the wind is blowing should be taken into account to prevent the chance of your shelter flying away.

- The ground should be comfortable enough if you plan to get some sleep. Pointy rocks will keep you awake.

- The ground should slope slightly for any water to run off. If there is no slope and rain is likely, you will need to dig some trenches around your shelter to aid drainage.

- Take into account the purpose of the shelter, and make it as large as it needs to be.

- Consider the weather and choose a design that is stable and won't collapse if rain or snow is heavy.

- An A-frame shelter is made by stringing paracord or rope between two trees, draping the tarp over it, and staking it down.

- A sunshade shelter needs four anchoring points to which you tie the paracord. The shelter is parallel to the ground and provides 100 square feet of shade and shelter from rain.

- A lean-to shelter is secured to the ground on the windward side and supported with the paracord between two anchor points. It is set at a 30-degree angle and is easy to erect and take down.

- A tube tent shelter provides a floor. It is draped over paracord tied between two trees.

- A mushroom fly shelter is similar to the sunshade but adds a central support pole at the tarp's midpoint. It is best for rain or snow runoff.

- A corner shelter starts with paracord strung from a tree to the ground and staked, then the tarp is draped over the cord, with a third of the tarp forming a floor.

- A diamond fly tarp is the simple version of a corner shelter without the floor.

- Other possible (more complicated) designs are the arrowhead shelter, the barn stall shelter, the dining fly shelter, the shade sail shelter, the square arch shelter, and the wind shed shelter. These take research, guidance, and practice.

- Don't build a shelter over a burrow, insect nest, or other nest.

- Don't set up your shelter beneath a dead tree or in the vicinity of one. To avoid being the main target of lightning, don't attach tarp lines to a tree standing alone or to tall trees. Always go for the short tree in a group of taller trees. Also don't set up your shelter on top of a hill or ridge.

- Don't set up your shelter below the high-tide mark of a shoreline or on a riverbank.

MAKING A FIRE

- Collect and prepare materials to start and feed a fire.

- Dry wood of all different sizes should be gathered first.

- You'll need tinder—some kind of dry, flammable material. Paper and birch or cedar bark are good options.

- If you failed to bring a firestarter (waterproof matches, lighter, or other spark-producing devices), you will have to resort to making a friction fire, which is not as simple as rubbing two sticks together. Learn the technique first (instructional videos can be found online). If you've never started a friction fire, you're unlikely to successfully do so in a survival situation.

- Hopefully you did remember to pack a knife!

- The first component of a friction fire, a fireboard or hearth, is a board or piece of dry, dead wood that you carve to be flat and just a few inches thick. Placed on the ground, the fireboard is the object that produces sawdust and eventually a coal when bored into by the spindle.

- The spindle (or drill) is a round, straight wooden stick that usually measures about an inch in diameter. The length can vary from 8 to 24 inches. If especially short or long, it may be hard to handle. One end is carved to be slightly tapered, coming to a point at the center.

- A bow is used to spin the spindle. To make this item, you'll need a long, skinny but strong branch that's relatively straight and about the length of your arm. Cordage is fastened to each end, spanning between in a tight line. You can simply wrap the cordage around one end so you can readjust the tautness of the line as needed.

FUN FACT

Nineteenth-century hiking was embedded within routines of berry picking, picnicking, traveling, hunting, and even professional tasks, such as surveying.

- The next component is a handhold or bearing block, which is an object that's held at the top of the spindle to keep it upright and in place as it spins. This is sometimes carved out of green wood, which is less likely to burn. It can also be made of clay, or you can find a stone that's the right shape to hold the top of the spindle. With a circular indent in the center for the spindle, it's held on top of the spindle by your nondominant hand.

- The last component needed is a small, flat piece of material to catch the sawdust and ember created by the bow drill. This can be a green leaf, a flat stone, or anything that will not burn quickly. This is placed under the fireboard, directly under where you are spinning the spindle.

- To start, carve a small circle or divot in the fireboard near the edge. Place the spindle in the divot, then use the bow to spin the spindle back and forth, burning a hole into the board with friction.

- To use the bow, wrap its cord once around the spindle so it's held tightly and the cord is taut between the two ends of the bow. Then, with the spindle standing with one end in the divot on the fireboard and the other end held by the handhold, saw the bow back and forth parallel to the ground. The spindle spins as it moves from one end of the bow to the other.

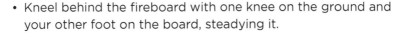

- Kneel behind the fireboard with one knee on the ground and your other foot on the board, steadying it.

- Once a circle has been burned into the fireboard, carve a V-shaped notch from the center of the circle to the edge of the board. This makes a slot for the sawdust to fall through and collect on the coal catcher.

- Continue to spin the spindle in its hole on the fireboard, creating enough friction to drill into the board and form a pile of sawdust and, eventually, build up enough heat to light that dust and form an ember.

- The ember is coaxed to life with oxygen. Once burning red, transfer it to a nest-shaped bundle of tinder. If blown on gently, the bundle should quickly burst into flame.

- All that's left to do is build up the fire with your kindling, starting with tiny sticks and working your way up to larger pieces of wood.

WHEN WE ALLOW OURSELVES TO EXPLORE,
WE DISCOVER DESTINATIONS THAT
WERE NEVER ON OUR MAP.
—AMIE KAUFMAN

WHEN TO WAIT FOR RESCUE AND WHEN TO HIKE OUT

WAIT FOR RESCUE:

- If someone will quickly notice you have not returned when due and you left a trip plan with them.

- You are prepared to spend the night.

- Rainy or cold weather threatens and you have a warm shelter.

- You are injured or beyond tired.

- You cannot move without risking injury or worse.

- Not much daylight remains.

- You are unsure of your location or which direction to hike.

- You are on a popular trail and have already seen other hikers.

- When in doubt, call for help.

HIKE OUT WHEN:

- No one knows where you are and you did not leave a trip plan with anyone.

- You are prepared to hike.

- You can handle the trails and terrain.

- Few people hike in the area.

- You lack warm clothing or shelter for spending the night.

- Rainy or cold weather threatens and you do not have a warm shelter.

- Several hours of good visibility remain.

- You have a map and compass and/or GPS and know how to use them, and you recognize terrain features or landmarks.

HIKING IN A PANDEMIC

- Hopefully, as you are reading this book we have moved beyond the pandemic. This section is included in the event there is a national emergency in the future. Scores of people discovered the joy of hiking during the pandemic. Follow the tips below to safely recreate outdoors during a similar situation.

  - You should go outside and get fresh air and exercise. Being outside in nature provides physical and mental benefits.

  - Time outdoors is often designated as an "essential activity" in many areas, but check local regulations before heading out.

- If you can, try to head out during off-hours.

- Stay local, and avoid driving to major recreation areas that are attractions for large groups. During a period when people have more downtime, trails can be filled with new hikers, runners, and cyclists.

- Look for less popular trails in your community; maybe you'll stumble on a hidden gem.

- Do not seek out technical trails. Reconsider your travel plans if you had a long-distance trip planned to a remote area.

- Do not go on a thru-hike that involves the use of picnic tables, privies, hiker huts/shelters, hostels, trail volunteers, communities close to or on the trail, and so on.

- Bring a mask or whatever is recommended in case you cannot avoid close contact with others.

- Realize that you must plan extremely well so you don't run into unsafe situations. From public restrooms to gas stations to food and supply needs, it is better to take the time to plan and be prepared. It is not a time to take unnecessary risks.

- If a trailhead parking lot is full, the trail likely will be, too. Consider finding another place to go if the lot is overcrowded.

FUN FACT

The first Saturday in June is National Trails Day in the United States.

- Avoid singletrack trails, as it is difficult to keep your distance when passing others. Instead, opt for wide trails or fire roads that can accommodate more people.

- Look for loop trails as a preference to out-and-back trails. Not everyone will necessarily be headed in the same direction, but there's a good chance you'll encounter less return traffic on a loop than on an out-and-back.

- Only venture out with people in your household or by yourself.

- Overcommunicate while on the trail, and announce yourself to others when passing to help maintain separation.

  - Be safe, but be kind. Some hikers may be slower than you, and some may not be as familiar with the trail.

  - Be patient with one another, but help remind your community of the importance of social distancing, even while outdoors.

- It is more important than ever in a pandemic or other emergency situation that you act as a responsible steward of outdoor places. Absolutely follow Leave No Trace principles.

WILDERNESS FIRST-AID BASICS

This section offers a cursory overview of common injuries and first aid. All hikers should take the time to complete an online and/or in-person wilderness first-aid course.

Such a course will teach patient assessment and what to do for chest injuries, shock, head and spinal injuries, bone and joint injuries, wounds and wound infection, allergies and anaphylaxis, abdominal problems, hypothermia, heat-related illness, lightning strikes, altitude sickness, and water submersion.

No matter your level of training, you need a complete first-aid kit with instructions for first aid as well as the Heimlich maneuver and CPR.

The order of steps: Size up the scene, identify any life threats, do a focused exam (head-to-toe check, vital signs, patient history), make a problem list and care plan (including evacuation decision), treat and monitor the patient.

- **Abdominal pain:** Assume the fetal position to relax abdominal muscles. Drink fluids and eat bland foods. Evacuate if pain persists, blood in urine, or fever. Possibly take antacid.

- **Blisters:** Apply blister pack if early on. Otherwise, clean with soap and water, then pop with a sterilized needle, tweezers, or knife. Apply antibiotic ointment and bandage.

- **Broken or dislocated bone:** Immobilize and pad the injured area. Evacuate if victim can walk; otherwise call for help.

- **Burns:** Run cold water over burn for 10 minutes. Apply antibiotic ointment and wrap with gauze. Evacuate if red lines trail away from injured area.

- **Cuts and scrapes:** Flush with water. If bleeding, hold gauze over wound and apply firm pressure. When bleeding stops, apply antibiotic ointment and bandage.

- **Flu-like illness:** Rest and stay hydrated. Evacuate if fever over 102 for more than 48 hours, headache with stiff neck, or difficulty swallowing. Possibly take ibuprofen or acetaminophen.

- **Frostnip and frostbite:** Rewarm mild cases with skin-to-skin contact in an armpit or groin. Immerse frostbite in water just above body temperature until all numbness fades, then bandage in gauze. Evacuate in all but the mildest cases. Possibly take ibuprofen.

- **Genital or urinary issues:** Stay well-hydrated. Possibly take an over-the-counter drug for urinary tract infection or antifungal for yeast infection. Evacuate to avoid worsening or spreading infection.

- **Nausea, vomiting, diarrhea:** Rest and hydrate, including with electrolytes, and wait it out (24 to 48 hours). Evacuate if cramping pain lasts more than 24 hours, fever, or cannot keep liquids down. Possibly take Pepto-Bismol, acetaminophen, or Imodium.

- **Poisonous plant allergic reaction:** Wash the area as soon as possible. Use Tecnu, a skin cleanser, to wash off poisonous oils. Avoid scratching. Evacuate if rash or blisters are oozing, swelling, or show spreading red lines. Possibly use topical cortisone or antihistamine for itching.

- **Snakebite:** Stay calm; any activity can increase absorption of venom. Clean the wound with soap. Limit activity by having someone help carry the victim out. Get to a medical facility as soon as possible.

- **Strains and sprains:** (a sprain is a stretch or tear of a ligament, while a strain is an injury to a muscle or tendon): Reduce swelling by soaking the injury in a cold river or lake, or applying ice or a cool damp cloth. Wrap in an elastic bandage. Massage and gently stretch a muscle injury. Elevate limb above the heart during rest. Possibly take ibuprofen or acetaminophen for pain.

- **Tooth problem:** Bite down on gauze if bleeding; flush with treated water. Cover with gauze. Evacuate to save a lost tooth or if signs of infection.

FIRST-AID KIT

- adhesive and butterfly bandages
- adhesive tape
- alcohol swabs
- antacid
- antibiotic ointment
- antihistamine cream
- antiseptic ointment
- antiseptic soap
- aspirin, acetaminophen, or ibuprofen
- blister plasters, moleskin
- bulb irrigating syringe
- burn ointment
- cellular telephone
- chemical cold and heat packs
- cotton balls/cotton swabs
- diarrhea medicine
- duct tape
- elastic wrap/Ace bandage
- epinephrine kits and antihistamine tablets
- first-aid manual
- gauze pads
- ground sheet
- hi-vis jacket or shirt
- hydrocortisone cream
- hydrogen peroxide
- insect repellent

- matches
- medication alert
- mild laxative
- mild sedative
- mirror, small and unbreakable
- motion-sickness medication
- paper cups/measuring spoons
- personal prescriptions
- poison-ivy medication
- razor blades
- rubbing alcohol
- safety pins
- salt tablets, electrolyte powders
- sugar packets, salt packets
- scissors or Swiss Army knife with scissors
- sheet/towels/blanket
- smelling salts
- snakebite kit (freeze kit)
- splints
- sterile gauze pads, two sizes
- sunscreen
- tourniquet
- triangular bandage
- tweezers/tick remover, needle and thread
- water purification tablets
- wet wipes

FIRST-AID INSTRUCTIONS

This information is not intended as a substitute for professional medical advice, emergency treatment, or formal first-aid training. Don't use this information to diagnose or develop a treatment plan for a health problem or disease without consulting a qualified health-care provider. If you're in a life-threatening or emergency medical situation, seek medical assistance immediately.

FIRST-AID LIFESAVING SEQUENCE

Evaluation:

- Size up the scene.

- Identify life threats.

- Do a focused exam: head-to-toe check, vital signs, and patient history.

- Make a problem list and care plan, which includes an evacuation decision.

- Treat the patient, providing both medical and emotional support.

- Monitor how the patient is doing.

Preparation:

- Determine whether the area is safe: Ensure no further harm is imminent—for both patient and responders. If a rockslide caused the injury, for example, you might need to move the patient out of the path of additional rockfall.

- Identify the mechanism of injury (MOI). Look around to determine what might have caused the accident or injury. This provides clues to the type of injuries that might be present.

- Form a general impression of the seriousness of the situation. If the patient is injured, how injured? If the person is sick, how sick?

- Determine the number of patients. Don't assume that the most obviously injured person is the only one in need of assessment and care.

- Protect yourself: Prudent caregiver practice is to assume all people are infectious. Put on gloves and a mask, and wash hands thoroughly before and after patient contact.

INITIAL PATIENT ASSESSMENT

- Obtain consent to treat (if the person is conscious). Ask the person if you can help. If the answer is "yes," then ask their name, symptoms, and what happened.

- Establish responsiveness. Attempt to wake the patient if they aren't responding. (If there is any possibility of a spine injury, you also need to carefully place your hands on either side of the person's head and keep the patient still.)

- Airway check: Look in the mouth and check the airway for obstructions.

- Breathing check: Look closely at the chest; listen and feel for signs of respiration.

- Circulation check: Check for a pulse and for major wounds that are bleeding.

- Disability decision: If you can't rule out a spine injury, continue to protect it.

- Expose injuries: Without moving the patient, open up clothing covering serious injuries so you can fully evaluate and treat them.

SECONDARY PATIENT ASSESSMENT

Head-to-Toe Exam:

- Look: for blood and other bodily fluids, discoloration, or unusual shapes.

- Listen: for airway noises or unusual sounds when joints are moved.

- Feel: for wounds, deformities and unexpected hardness, softness, or tenderness.

- Smell: for unusual odors.

- Ask: if anything hurts or feels odd or numb.

Check Vital Signs:

- Level of responsiveness: Is the patient awake and oriented? Awake and disoriented? Or unconscious or unresponsive?

- Heart rate: Using the wrist pulse, check the number of beats per minute and note whether the pulse is strong or weak, regular or irregular.

- Respiration rate: Check the patient's number of breaths per minute and note whether the breathing is easy or labored.

- Skin signs: Look at skin color, temperature, and moisture. The inside rim of the lower eye or inside the lower lip are good places to check for color. Is it pink or pale? Is the rest of their skin warm and dry vs. cool and clammy? If possible, also record the patient's temperature with a thermometer.

Do a Patient History:

- Chief complaint: Ask the following questions: What is your most significant concern? When did it start? What makes it worse or better? Where is it located? How severe is it?

- How old is the patient?

- Symptoms: Ask if the patient can provide additional details about the chief complaint, or if they have other conditions or concerns.

- Allergies: Are there severe ones? (Food and medicine are common ones; also ask about bees.) What are the patient's reactions to their allergies?

- Medications: Get as many details as possible for both prescription and over-the-counter drugs.

- Pertinent medical history: Find out if they have any medical conditions that require them to see a doctor for treatment.

- Last fluid/food intake, last urine/bowel output: How long ago and how much?

- Events: Ask if they know what caused the event and the details leading up to it.

Tips:

- If possible, have someone of the same gender perform the head-to-toe exam.

- Have someone help the examiner by writing down observations and vital signs.

- Assign other tasks, like boiling water for drinks or setting up camp, so that the patient feels like care is orderly and all rescuers have a role.

- Try to keep the patient clean, warm, and comfortable at all times. If you are waiting for help to arrive, things like shelter, sustenance, and general nursing care will be key to maintaining patient well-being.

- Fluids are more important than food; avoid caffeinated and sugary drinks.

- Offer emotional support and empathy.

- Inform the patient about all aspects of care and involve them in evacuation decisions.

- Resupply and/or supplement your first-aid kit before each trip (consider a larger tube of antibiotic ointment or more dressing materials, among other things).

ALLERGIC REACTION, MILD

- Take an antihistamine such as Benadryl.

- Avoid scratching, as this will further irritate the rash, increase the risk of infection, and cause scarring.

- Apply cornstarch packs to reduce the itching of hives.

- Apply a thin layer of steroid cream, such as hydrocortisone, to rashes caused by allergens rubbed against the skin.

- Apply calamine lotion to poison oak and insect bites. Steroid cream may also be effective with poison oak.

ALLERGIC REACTION, SEVERE

- Know in advance what your companions are allergic to and where they keep their inhalers, epinephrine kits, and allergy medications. Consider wearing a medic alert bracelet if you know you are susceptible to anaphylactic shock.

- Learn to identify the signs and symptoms of anaphylaxis: difficulty breathing, wheezing, rash, itching, hives, swelling of the feet, hands, eyes, or face, flushed skin, nausea, vomiting, abdominal pain, rapid pulse.

- Remove the person from contact with the allergen if the allergen is suspected to be something in the air or on the skin.

- Administer injectable epinephrine (adrenaline) immediately if the person is having difficulty talking or breathing. Epinephrine is usually prescribed in an Anakit or EpiPen with a preloaded syringe, and is injected intramuscularly in the thigh for rapid absorption.

- Monitor airway, breathing, and circulation.

- Treat for shock.

- Inject a second dose of epinephrine within 12 to 15 minutes after the first dose was administered to prevent a relapse. Most kits contain at least two doses.

- Administer an oral antihistamine once the epinephrine has taken effect and the person is able to take the medication on their own.

- Hydrate well.

- Evacuate immediately, administering oral antihistamines at regular intervals until the person has reached professional medical care.

BANDAGING A WOUND

- Protect yourself. Scrub your hands thoroughly with soap and disinfected water, and put on medical gloves to prevent the spread of infectious disease.

- Clean the wound and carefully remove any excess debris.

- Remove any jewelry, such as rings or watches, that might impair circulation.

- Apply antibiotic cream to the inside of the material you are using as a dressing.

- Cover the wound with the dressing. The dressing should extend beyond the wound by about ½ inch so that it covers the wound completely and allows room to affix the dressing to uninjured skin.

- Cut four strips of adhesive tape and affix them to the dressing and skin on all four sides of the dressing. The purpose of the bandage is to help keep the dressing in place, and it shouldn't be too loose (able to move around) or too tight (impairing circulation).

- If there is a risk that the wound will be exposed to water, cover the bandage with waterproof material such as waterproof tape or plastic.

- Look at and feel the area and limb surrounding the wound to make certain the dressing does not impair circulation.

- Ask the injured person if they can feel the area you are touching, feel no pain or tingling, and can move the limb fully. The skin should be pink and slightly warm to the touch.

BITE FROM ANIMAL

- Move away from the animal and ensure the safety of the scene to prevent additional bites.

- Put on medical gloves as protection from infectious disease.

- Clean the wound thoroughly and aggressively with an antiseptic soap or povidone-iodine solution.

- Keep the wound open—do not attempt to close it with closure strips or butterfly bandages.

- Dress and bandage the wound.

- Keep the patient well-hydrated.

- Monitor carefully for infection.

- Evacuate immediately to a hospital, regardless of whether or not you believe the animal was rabid.

BITE FROM INSECT

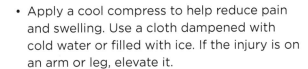

- Wash the area with soap and water.

- Apply a cool compress to help reduce pain and swelling. Use a cloth dampened with cold water or filled with ice. If the injury is on an arm or leg, elevate it.

- Apply 0.5 or 1 percent hydrocortisone cream, calamine lotion, or a baking soda paste to the bite or sting several times daily until symptoms go away.

- Take an antihistamine (Benadryl, others) to reduce itching.

- If the signs and symptoms do not disappear in a few days or if you are concerned, get medical help.

BITE FROM SNAKE

- Move away from the snake and ensure safety of the scene to prevent additional bites.

- Calm the patient down and keep them still and quiet.

- Elevate the bite at or below the level of the heart.

- Remove any jewelry or other articles that may constrict with swelling.

- Suction immediately with a Sawyer Extractor, ideally within 3 minutes after the patient has been bit.

- If extractor not available: Apply hard direct pressure over bite using a 4 x 4 gauze pad folded in half twice. Soak gauze pad in antiseptic soap or solution if available. Strap gauze pad tightly in place with adhesive tape.

- Overwrap dressing above and below bite area with an Ace or crepe bandage, but not too tightly—no tighter than you would use for a sprain. Check for pulse above and below elastic wrap; if absent it is too tight. Unpin and loosen.

- Immobilize the extremity, and splint if possible.

- Keep the patient well-hydrated.

- Evacuate immediately, preferably without any effort on the part of the patient. An ideal evacuation would involve sending others to arrange for a helicopter evacuation. Get the patient to the hospital immediately.

BITE FROM SPIDER

- Clean the wound. Use mild soap and water and apply an antibiotic ointment.

- Apply a cool compress to help reduce pain and swelling. Use a cloth dampened with cold water or filled with ice. If the bite is on an arm or leg, elevate it.

- Take an over-the-counter pain medication if needed. If the wound is itchy, an antihistamine (Benadryl, Chlor-Trimeton, or similar) may help.

BLEEDING, STOPPING

- Elevate the injured area above the heart.

- Apply direct pressure to the bleeding area, using sterile cloth or gauze.

- Keep the pressure on for 5 minutes.

- Check to see if the bleeding has stopped. If it hasn't, apply pressure for 15 minutes.

BLISTER

- Try to keep a blister intact by covering it with a bandage or using a piece of moleskin cut into a doughnut shape to encircle the blister and give it air.

- Seek medical care if a blister looks infected.

BURN

- Remove the source of the burn: For flame burns, stop, drop, and roll; for wet chemical burns, flush the area with water for 20 minutes; for dry chemical burns, brush off the dry chemicals.

- Remove any clothing and jewelry, since they retain heat and can exacerbate burning.

- Check airway, breathing, and circulation. Treat with rescue breathing and/or CPR as necessary.
- Cool the burn with cold (but warmer than ice-cold) water, or with cloths dampened with cold water.
- Assess the depth and extent of the burn.
- Elevate the burn site above the heart.
- Have the injured person drink as much as possible, unless they are unconscious and/or showing signs of shock.
- Clean the burn area gently with disinfected lukewarm water and mild soap. Pat dry, then flush any debris out with an irrigation syringe. Pat dry again.
- Apply a thin layer of antibiotic ointment to the burn site with a cotton swab.
- Cover the burn with dry, sterile gauze.
- Give ibuprofen to reduce pain and swelling.
- Evacuate unless only minor superficial burns are involved.
- Re-dress the burn twice a day on the hike out: Remove the dressing (which may require soaking it first), rewash the burn site, reapply antibiotic ointment, and re-dress with gauze.

CLEANING A WOUND

- Scrub hands thoroughly with soap and disinfected water.
- Put on medical gloves to prevent the spread of infectious disease.
- Prepare a disinfectant solution of 1 ounce povidone-iodine and 1 liter disinfected water.
- Set the disinfectant solution aside for about 5 minutes.

CPR

- Determine if the surrounding scene is safe.

- If not in a wilderness setting, tell someone nearby to call 911.

- Determine if the injured person is breathing.

- Position the injured person on their back, being extremely careful not to move or twist the head, neck, or spine. If several rescuers are present, use their assistance to minimize this danger.

- Maintain an open airway while you pinch the injured person's nose shut.

- Give two long, slow breaths, being sure to maintain a seal between your mouth and the patient's mouth.

- Begin CPR if the person is neither breathing nor has a pulse.

- Position the hands: Find the lower tip of the breastbone. Measure two finger widths toward the head, and place the heel of one hand in this location.

- Place your other hand on top of the first hand, interlacing the fingers of both hands.

- Lean forward so that your shoulders are over your hands.

- Push downward on the chest, using the weight of your upper body for strength. Compress fifteen times in 10 seconds.

- Give two more slow breaths after the fifteen compressions.

- Do fifteen more compressions followed again by two slow breaths.

- Perform the fifteen-compression/two-breath cycle a total of four times.

- Recheck for pulse and breathing.

- Continue repeating this entire cycle—four sets of chest compressions and breaths followed by rechecking pulse and breathing—until the injured person regains a pulse, professional medical help arrives, or you are too exhausted to continue.

CRAMP

- Move the person out of direct sunlight, preferably into a cool, shaded area.

- Stretch the calf and thigh muscles gently through the cramp. This will usually bring immediate relief.

- Hydrate well, preferably with a diluted sports drink or oral rehydration solution. A teaspoon of salt in a liter of water will also work.

- Have the person rest quietly.

FROSTBITE, MILD

- Consider taking a pain reliever such as ibuprofen to brace for the inevitable pain of rewarming.

- Gather the following supplies if possible: a camp stove with fuel, a pot in which to heat water, a receptacle large enough to hold the affected body part without allowing it to touch the sides, and a thermometer to check the water's temperature.

- Heat the right amount of water—enough to cover the affected area once it's in the receptacle—to between 104 and 108 degrees F.

- Pour the heated water into the receptacle.

- Immerse the affected part—stripped of all clothing and covering—in the water, taking care that it doesn't touch the sides of the receptacle.

- Heat more water, again to between 104 and 108 degrees F.

- Replace the water in the receptacle once it has cooled to below 100 degrees F.

- Repeat the heat-and-replace cycle until all discoloration has disappeared and the tissue is once again soft and pliable. This usually takes 30 to 60 minutes.

- Prepare a bath of water mixed with antibacterial soap. Immerse the affected area for 5 minutes to minimize risk of infection.

- Air-dry the injured area and gingerly apply aloe vera ointment.

- Cover the injured area gently with dry sterile gauze and insulating layers.

- Evacuate if you are outdoors, taking extreme care not to let the frostbitten body part refreeze.

FROSTBITE, SEVERE

- Figure out if it's possible to evacuate without the affected area being used. For instance, can the person be moved without walking on a frostbitten foot?

- Decide if you'll be able to keep the person, including the affected area, warm throughout the eventual evacuation.

- Determine if you have all the supplies for field rewarming: the ability to heat a lot of water for a long time, a receptacle large enough to hold the affected part without allowing it to touch the sides, and a thermometer to check the water's temperature.

- Rewarm in the field only if the above three conditions are met: no necessity to use the affected area before reaching a hospital, ability to keep the person warm during the evacuation, and adequate supplies to rewarm properly. Otherwise, evacuate before rewarming.

HEAT EXHAUSTION

- Evaluate for heat exhaustion. If you suspect heat exhaustion, treat with the following steps:

- Move the person out of direct sunlight, preferably into a cool, shaded area.

- If the person feels dizzy or has fainted suddenly, have them lie flat and elevate their feet.

- Have the person rest quietly.

- Move to a cool, shaded area.

- Hydrate well with lots of water or a diluted sports drink or oral rehydration solution.

- Remove heat-retaining clothing.

- Wet the person down and fan them with a shirt or towel.

- Place a wet bandanna or thin strip of cotton cloth on the person's forehead, top of the head, or back of the neck.

- Monitor body temperature frequently. If it rises to above 104 degrees, aggressively cool the person.

HEATSTROKE

- Evaluate for heatstroke. Warning signs vary but may include high temperature (over 103 degrees), red-hot dry skin with no sweating, rapid strong pulse, throbbing headache, dizziness, nausea, confusion, and unconsciousness. If you suspect heatstroke, treat with the following steps:

- Move the patient out of direct sunlight, preferably into a cool, shaded area.

- Have the patient lie flat and elevate their feet.

- Remove heat-retaining clothing.

- Wet the patient down and fan them, or immerse the patient in cool water.

- Place ice packs on the patient's head, back of the neck, armpits, palms of the hands or soles of the feet, and groin.

- Hydrate well with lots of water or a diluted sports drink or oral rehydration solution, but only if the patient is conscious enough to hold a cup and drink unassisted.

- Monitor body temperature frequently, keeping careful notes on how long the patient remains at a given temperature. Transfer these notes when you transfer care.

- Evacuate immediately, continually monitoring and writing down the patient's body temperature.

HEIMLICH MANEUVER

The Heimlich maneuver is an emergency procedure to help someone who is choking because food is lodged in the trachea. To perform abdominal thrusts (Heimlich maneuver) on someone else:

• Stand behind the person. Place one foot slightly in front of the other for balance. Wrap your arms around their waist. Tip the person forward slightly. If a child is choking, kneel down behind the child.

• Make a fist with one hand. Position it slightly above the person's navel.

• Grasp the fist with the other hand. Press hard into the abdomen with a quick, upward thrust—as if trying to lift the person up.

• Perform between six and ten abdominal thrusts until the blockage is dislodged.

HYPOTHERMIA, MILD

• Remove the affected person from the cold, wet, and/or windy environment.

• Dry the person off, replacing wet clothing with dry clothing.

• Shelter the person however possible: in a cave, under an overhang, in an improvised shelter such as a tent or under a rain fly.

• Make sure the person is wearing a dry hat: A large percentage of body-heat loss occurs through the head.

• Cover their neck with something dry: A lot of heat is also lost through the neck.

• If you have a camp stove, prepare a warm (not hot) beverage and have the hypothermic person drink it.

• Encourage the person to eat carbohydrate-rich foods.

• Encourage the person to move around, which generates heat and helps with rewarming.

HYPOTHERMIA, MODERATE

• Remove the affected person from the cold, wet, and/or windy environment.

- Dry the person off, replacing wet clothing with dry clothing.

- Shelter the person however possible: in a cave, under an overhang, in an improvised shelter such as a tent or under a rain fly.

- Make sure the person is wearing a dry hat: A large percentage of body-heat loss occurs through the head.

- Cover their neck with something dry: A lot of heat is also lost through the neck.

- Insulate the person from the ground and the surrounding cold by having them lie in a sleeping bag on a sleeping pad.

- If you have a camp stove, prepare a warm (not hot) beverage and have the hypothermic person drink it.

- Encourage the person to eat carbohydrate-rich foods.

- Place hot water bottles (filled with hot water) and/or chemical heat packs inside the sleeping bag and against the clothing of the hypothermic person.

- Build a fire near the person, but take care that it isn't close enough to risk catching anything on fire.

- Monitor closely for changes in level of consciousness: A worsening condition may indicate severe hypothermia.

HYPOTHERMIA, SEVERE

- Remove the affected person from the cold, wet, and/or windy environment.

- Dry the person off, replacing wet clothing with dry clothing.

- Shelter the person however possible: in a cave, under an over-hang, in an improvised shelter such as a tent or under a rain fly.

- Make sure the person is wearing a dry hat: A large percentage of body-heat loss occurs through the head.

- Cover their neck with something dry: A lot of heat is also lost through the neck.

- Insulate the person from the ground and the surrounding cold by having them lie in a sleeping bag on a sleeping pad.

- Place hot water bottles (filled with hot water) and/or chemical heat packs inside the sleeping bag and against the clothing of the hypothermic person.

- Build a "hypothermia wrap" by placing dry clothing over all exposed parts of the person except their mouth and nose, and wrap a vapor barrier—a tent fly, plastic garbage bags, anything that will minimize the escape of heat—around the person.

MUSCLE PULL OR STRAIN

- Apply an ice pack for 20 minutes to any area that hurts. Repeat this every hour until the pain subsides.

- Stretch the sore area gently to rid your body of lactic acid, which contributes to the pain.

- Avoid strenuous activity as long as you're in pain.

POISONOUS PLANT

- Immediately wash everything that might have touched the plant. You may be able to take off the offending oil completely or at least reduce the impending rash.

- Soothe itching with cool, wet compresses.

- Apply lotion containing calamine, alcohol, and zinc acetate; these will dry the blisters and help speed healing.

- Leave a rash open to the air to help it heal.

- Remember that toxic oils from poisonous plants need to be washed out of clothes before wearing them again.

SPRAIN

- Rest the injured limb. Get emergency assistance if you are unable to bear weight on the injured leg, the joint seems unstable or is numb, or you cannot use the joint at all. This may indicate a torn ligament.

- Ice the area. Use a cold pack, a slush bath, or a compression sleeve filled with cold water to help limit swelling after an injury. Try to ice the area as soon as possible after the injury and continue to ice it for 15 to 20 minutes, four to eight times a day, for the first 48 hours or until swelling improves. If you use ice, be careful not to use it too long, as this could cause tissue damage.

- Compress the area with an elastic wrap or bandage. Compression wraps or sleeves made from elastic or neoprene are best.

- Elevate the injured limb above your heart whenever possible to help prevent or limit swelling.

TICK REMOVAL

- Check your naked body from head to toe for ticks—small black, brown, reddish, or tan disklike arachnids (having eight legs) that range from the size of a pinhead to almost the size of a thumbtack. Pay special attention to the backs of your knees, your groin area, and your torso.

- Ask a friend or family member for help if you find a tick in a hard-to-reach spot.

- Hold (or have the other person hold) a pair of tweezers in one hand and grasp the tick with the tweezers close to the surface of your skin. Avoid grabbing the body of the tick with your fingers and trying to pull it out. You might leave some parts of the tick under your skin and also expose your hands to any disease the tick is carrying.

- Gently but firmly pull the tick straight out, working for several seconds if necessary until it loosens and comes free. Occasionally, parts of the tick's mouth become separated from the rest of the tick; if they do, pull them out separately.

- Dispose of the tick by throwing it into a fire, or by squishing it using a tissue and then flushing it down the toilet. Don't smash it with your foot or bare hands.

- Clean the bite site thoroughly with soap and water or Betadine, and thoroughly wash your hands.

WEATHER AND WILDLIFE

THE BEST WEATHER INSTRUMENT YET
DEVISED IS A PAIR OF HUMAN EYES.
—HAROLD M. GIBSON

TWO FACTORS THAT CAN GREATLY AFFECT A HIKE—BUT are also part of the fun of hiking—are weather and wildlife. You have heard how important it is to check the weather forecast from more than one resource. We've also covered the value of doing some research on what to expect as far as flora and fauna in the area of your planned adventure.

Weather and wildlife are two very changeable factors, so this chapter discusses some particular situations for which you can do additional planning and preparation. Look at it this way: If you were attending a social event, you'd likely want to know who might be there and what type of attire would be appropriate. Hiking is more fun (and safer!) when you have more information and knowledge, as well as the right clothing and gear.

WEATHER BASICS

- It is impossible to know what the weather will do, even on a day hike. Your motto is to be prepared.

- The first things to bring are common sense and caution. If there's any percent chance of rain, believe the meteorologists and carry reliable rain gear. If there's wind or other factors that could alter your comfort, wear layers of clothing.

- Beyond believing the forecast, investigate historical weather patterns if you are hiking in an unfamiliar area, such as if you are traveling and doing a hike. Contact rangers, locals, and online hiking communities and consult guidebooks.

- While on a backpacking trip, make sure you have a way of getting up-to-the-minute forecasts every day.

- The sky tells the story. The shapes and movements of the clouds give the best information about changes that are coming.

- The stronger the wind is, the colder the air feels. Check the windchill prediction before you head out.

- Relative humidity is the amount of moisture in the air divided by how much water the air can hold at that temperature. High humidity makes cold feel colder and heat feel hotter.

- Barometric pressure is the weight that air exerts on the Earth per unit area. If the barometric pressure is falling, the weather is likely worsening and a storm is coming. If the barometric pressure is rising, it indicates clearing and cooler weather.

- Warm fronts are air masses that gradually push out and replace cooler bodies of air. They move around half the speed of cold fronts and rarely produce violent weather. They can cause precipitation that may linger for a while. Learn how to recognize and read cirrus, cirrocumulus, cirrostratus, altostratus, nimbostratus, and stratus clouds.

- Cold fronts are air masses that slide in under warmer air pockets. They can develop and move fast. Temperatures drop, winds shift and pick up, and barometric pressure falls. Learn how to recognize and read cumulus and cumulonimbus clouds.

- An occluded front is a battle of three air masses; for example, when a fast-moving cold front overtakes a warm front, lifting (occluding) the warm air mass. The cold front then collides with the departing cold air mass. If the incoming cold front is warmer than the departing one, the new cold front climbs over the exiting one while trapping the warm front in the middle. If the incoming cold front is colder than the exiting one, it wedges under it. Storms are possible. Look for wind direction changes and falling then rising barometric pressure.

- If you know there will be a storm later in the day, get started as early as possible and cover as much ground as you can before the storm.

- Lightning is in all thunderstorms, since lightning causes thunder. If lightning threatens, take it seriously. Count the number of seconds between the flash of lightning in the sky and the sound of its thunder. Divide by 5 to figure the number of miles between you and the storm/ lightning. If your count was 10 seconds or less, the strike was within 2 miles. Seek shelter immediately.

- Stay away from any lone, tall object including trees. Descend from a peak, ridgeline, or high point. Head for lower ground and a less exposed area. The best place to be is within a group of trees of roughly uniform height in a low-lying area, or in a low spot in an open meadow.

- Stay away from water and out of shallow caves or overhangs. Separate yourself from metal or graphite objects like backpack frames, axes, crampons, and trekking poles.

- Insulate yourself from the ground with something rubber or a sleeping pad (ground current is usually the lethal force in lightning strikes). Crouch with your feet close together, even if you are on a pad.

- Research the effects of topography and other factors on weather. In the desert, the danger lies in thermals—columns of rising air that occur over hot spots. Air rushes to fill the column's low-pressure zone, spawning sandstorms with up to 75 mph winds. Be prepared and wear goggles, a windbreaker, and a bandanna or buff over your mouth and nose. Seek shelter.

THERE IS ALWAYS AN ADVENTURE WAITING IN THE WOODS.
—KATELYN S. BOLDS

COLD-WEATHER HIKING

- In colder weather, you need to wear the proper clothing, have essential gear, know what to eat and drink, and be prepared for cold-related injuries and illnesses.

- Choose clothing layers, starting with a base layer that wicks perspiration away from the skin, then a mid-layer that insulates you from the cold, and finally an outer/shell layer that keeps precipitation and wind out. In cold weather, you need to be able to add and remove layers to stay comfortable and warm.

- It may feel annoying to repeatedly take things off and put things on during a hike, but a bit of annoyance will save you from cold-related injuries and illnesses.

- Nothing should be too tight—watchband, cuffs of gloves or coat, gaiters, or footwear—because that causes poor circulation and increases your chance of frostbite.

- Know your body type related to temperature and how it changes in different types of weather and with different clothing. You don't want to be overheated and sweaty or freezing.

- Getting wet on a cold day can lead to hypothermia. That is why you don't wear cotton. When it gets wet, it takes a long time to dry compared with other fabrics and leaves the wet layer right on your skin, making you miserable and in danger.

- When temperatures are freezing, or the windchill (RealFeel) is freezing or below, you need to cover as much skin as possible (nose, cheeks, ears, fingers, toes) to prevent frostbite.

- Wear light- or mid-weight fleece gloves under waterproof shell mittens or gloves. Have extra gloves in case those get wet. Synthetic or wool socks are best, and you'll need an extra pair. Waterproof boots/shoes are great for hiking through snow. Leg gaiters help keep snow out of your footwear.

- For your head, a winter hat or headband can be accompanied by a neck gaiter (buff) or face mask. Protect your eyes from sun, wind, and cold with sunglasses or goggles. Use sunscreen and lip balm.

- Hike with the sun. As part of your Ten Essentials, pack a headlamp, since the days are shorter in winter. Keep batteries and electronics with batteries warm by carrying them in a pocket close to your body or wrapped inside those extra gloves and socks.

- Keep snacks and water within reach, and eat and drink regularly throughout the hike. You may not feel like stopping to eat, but you need food and liquids.

- In very cold temperatures, use a water bottle instead of a hydration reservoir because it has less chance of freezing. Flip it upside-down and keep it in your pack.

  - Consider packing a vacuum-insulated bottle with a hot beverage for sipping on breaks.

  - Become familiar with the signs of frostbite and hypothermia and how to treat these serious conditions. Focus on staying warm by dressing appropriately.

- If you feel your fingers and toes getting super cold, stop and assess, and warm them up in places like your armpits or groin—or use hand- or toe-warmer packets. Keep an eye on your partner or group, too.

- Some people love cold weather and others do not. The latter need to work a bit harder at developing their layering system and expanding their experience in cold-weather hiking.

- If a cold-weather hike is too much or the weather changes and makes it unbearable or too scary, just turn back.

HIKING IN SNOW

- Make sure the trail is open. Even if a park or reserve is open, specific trails may be closed based on conditions. A good hiking guide will list seasonal considerations and trail contacts to check with. If a trail is closed, do not enter. It also is best to hike with someone, not alone, in winter or in snow.

- Start out early and finish early; there's limited daylight in the winter. Be realistic about how much you can hike in a day. Ice and snow make trails much trickier.

- Consider the trail's topographical features and where the snow may be melting or freezing at different times of the day.

- Trekking poles are a must when hiking in snow. The extra contact points help steady you, and the poles are useful to find hidden banks and holes in the path.

  - An ice axe is also useful when hiking in snow. It can be used for support while ascending, for arresting your descent should you fall, or for cutting "steps" into hard-packed snow and ice.

  - Know when to use crampons. Crampons should only be used on hard-packed snow or ice. Do not use on loose or fresh snow.

- Snowshoes are used where snow is not heavily packed down. They help evenly distribute your weight over a larger surface area so you don't sink into the snow. Snowshoes should only be used in relatively flat areas because they do not grip the terrain well.

- Besides the Ten Essentials, pack gear for an unexpected overnight in the wilderness, such as a stove and fuel, flares, shelter, and space blanket. Hiking in snow is more risky than other hiking excursions.

- For snow and very cold temperatures, you might want to wear boots with built-in insulation. You can keep snow out of your boots with gaiters, which also add warmth. Be sure to get waterproof but breathable gaiters.

- The sun's rays reflect off the snow back up on you, so apply sunscreen under your nose and chin and on your neck. Sunglasses and/or goggles are not just protection from glare. If a squall or blizzard comes, you will not be able to see without them.

- Going uphill, take short steps and "kick into" the snowbank, called step-kicking. Use your boot to slice straight into the snow to create a level platform. Make sure your entire foot is in contact with the snow. Stand tall and center your weight over that foot. Try not to use kicked-in steps from previous travelers, as they may have turned icy.

- Look into using other uphill climbing steps such as duck foot, crossover step, and rest step. You can find good videos online to learn these steps.

- Going downhill, try plunge-stepping, a gravity-assisted step down, not forward. You do this by stepping away from the slope and firmly planting your heel into the snow. Keep your weight back, maintain a wide stance, and let gravity pull you toward your next step. Your stepping leg should be firm to resist the upward force of the slope to your foot. Avoid locking the knee.

- To get down a slope, you can also try glissading, either a seated glissade or standing glissade (boot skiing). You can find good videos online to learn these methods. Basically, think of it like sledding on your feet or behind without a sled. You can use trekking poles to control your balance and speed.

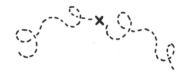

- Frozen bodies of water covered with snow and ice are very dangerous. Some may not be frozen enough to hold your weight.

- Watch out for overhangs or bluffs that could drop snow on you. If you are in higher elevations, stay below the tree line, which provides a natural protection barrier.

- If you are in a situation where hypothermia may be setting in, do whatever you can to get out of the wind and off the snow.

- Never question a feeling that you should "call it" while hiking and turn back or cancel the hike before starting out if the conditions are more than you can or want to handle.

COMBINE HIKING AND HISTORY:

- Find out if the trail includes an archaeological site and features.

- Learn the history of the trail.

- Learn the origin of the trail's name.

- Join a Friends group for your favorite trail.

HOT-WEATHER HIKING

- You may like hiking in warm weather, but with sun and humidity, heat can become intense. You need to know how to have fun and stay healthy in hot weather.

- Think about when and where you would like to hike. It takes about 10 to 14 days to acclimate to high heat, so start slowly and build up your experience as the days grow warmer.

- It is best to avoid hiking during the hottest part of the day. Depending on where you are, that is usually between noon and 3 p.m. Get an early start and end the hike by noon or early afternoon. Or start out after 3 p.m. in summer, since the sun does not go down until later.

- In popular areas, consider hiking at times when the crowds will not be there. Consider a night hike. If you live in or are visiting a very hot area, hiking at night can be a great option.

- Try to choose a hike that offers shade from trees or includes canyon walls or large stone walls and caves. Any area that is less exposed to the sun is cooler in summer.

- You can also hike near a body of water, which often provides a breeze. You can use a river or lake to splash water on yourself and your clothes, too.

- Wear light colors (white, khaki, tan) that reflect the sun's rays instead of absorb them. The fabric should be lightweight and the clothing loose-fitting; some items even incorporate vents. Nylon and polyester that are moisture-wicking are great options. Cotton is even okay in hot weather, but it will stay wet. If you like that feeling, cotton is fine. If it turns cool, though, cotton's wetness will chill you. Never wear cotton socks, though; stick with synthetic or wool.

- Consider UPF-rated clothing to gain more sun protection (UPF 15, 30, or 50+). But just wearing long sleeves, long pants, and a neck gaiter can provide adequate sun protection, too.

- Sunscreen is absolutely essential on hikes in the sun. Apply before you head out. When a hike is 2 hours or longer, get SPF 30 or higher. You'll need to reapply sunscreen around the 2-hour mark.

- Take care of your head and neck. Maybe choose a hat with a full brim instead of a cap, and use a bandanna or neck gaiter (buff) to pick up neck moisture.

- Lowering your body temperature in the hour before you hike in the heat slows the rate at which your core temperature rises once you're out the door. So try precooling before you head out.

- Water is key, so consider a hydration pack in hot weather. You can also carry a squirt/misting bottle with water.

- The general recommendation is 16 ounces (half liter) of water per hour of moderate activity in moderate temperatures; you'll need more in strenuous/hotter conditions. If you hike with a pet, they need water, too. Be careful not to overdo it and overdrink. Drink a few gulps of water about every 15 to 20 minutes.

- Keep your salt levels balanced by adding a sports drink with electrolytes and/or a salty snack or salt tablets. Pack food that will not spoil in hot weather. Stick with complex carbohydrates, trail mix, energy bars, and fruit.

- If you feel physical warning signs that you've pushed your limits, get out of the heat, rehydrate, and cool off. The best ways to prevent these problems are to acclimate slowly to hiking in hot weather and know what you can handle—your level of fitness plus your body's reaction to heat, humidity, and sweating.

- If you develop a throbbing headache, dizziness, nausea, vomiting, confusion, disorientation, or a temperature of 104 or higher, cool down and hydrate, then evacuate. Don't take a chance on heatstroke.

- Because mosquitoes and biting flies are most active at dawn and dusk, cover up your legs and arms if you are hiking at those times. When you rest or stop, stay in areas that are exposed to sunlight and breezes, because both of those deter swarming bugs.

- Insect repellent is important, so research and choose wisely. There is DEET and alternatives such as picaridin, citronella, and oil of lemon eucalyptus. There's bug-repellent clothing that lasts through many washings. Or you can spray clothing with permethrin to kill ticks and mosquitos, too.

COMBINE HIKING AND ART:

- Leave a painted kindness rock or rocks.

- Draw or paint a picture of the trailhead or scenic view.

- Take a photo at the start and end of every hiked trail.

- Take a photo of your hiker shadow on the trail.

- Create a photo montage of hiked trails at the end of the year.

MANAGING SWEAT

- Sweating is a completely normal response to the body heating, no matter what the source of the heat is. Sweat is a mixture of water, salt, and potassium that evaporates from your skin to cool you down, allowing your body to maintain its core temperature. It can be annoying—getting in your eyes, making your hands slippery, and just generally making you uncomfortable.

- High humidity prevents sweat from evaporating. The only real fix is to take it easy, slowing your pace. The more you train your body and the more time you exercise in hot, humid weather, the more efficient you become at sweating. Ironically, the more highly trained you are, the more you sweat, because your body has become efficient at cooling itself. A high fitness level allows you to exercise at a higher workload, which generates more heat and sweat.

- You cannot acclimate to exercise and heat if you do not drink enough water on a regular basis, including before you exercise.

- Genetics plays a major part in how much you sweat, which is largely determined before you turn 2 years old. Larger people sweat more because they work harder to carry a heavier load. And because muscle generates heat, if you have more muscle mass you may sweat more than a lean person.

- Eccrine sweat is a dilute sweat that occurs all over the body when it is hot outside, when you exercise, or both. How much eccrine sweat you produce is mostly determined by genetics, as is where you sweat. There are a lot of sweat glands in your forehead, spine, palms, and soles of your feet.

- Apocrine sweat is a fatty sweat created in the underarm and genital areas, which both have a density of sweat glands. Bacteria in skin digest the sweat and produce body odor.

FUN FACT

The rise of urban bicycle paths, rail trails, and other multiuse trail development, which began in the 1960s but accelerated in the 1990s, led to the development of thousands of miles of new hiking trails.

- Personal hydration and medication also influence how much you sweat. Other factors are gender, age, exercise intensity, body size, environmental temperature, ventilation and airflow, humidity, and breathability of clothing fabric.

- People view sweating as a bad thing, but it is the evaporation of sweat that enables you to not overheat. In high humidity or with low airflow, your sweat evaporates more slowly, preventing the cooling effect and possibly making you sweat more.

- Sweating a lot during exercise can cause dehydration, so it is important to replenish fluids through drinking. When exercising, most adults can comfortably and safely take in 50 ounces (1.5 liters) of water per hour.

- Opt for workout clothes with wicking properties. Go for high-tech synthetic fabrics that feel airy and wick moisture away from your skin.

- Try using a headband, wristband(s), or handkerchief or bandanna to wipe your face. You can also buy cooling neck cloths. Simply tying a wet handkerchief or bandanna around your neck may cool you down.

- Opt for antiperspirant (unscented). Apply before bed at night and reapply in the morning for best results. You could put antiperspirant on your hairline or other body parts, but when you block sweat glands in one part of the body, sweat glands in other parts of the body work harder. And if the antiperspirant gets into your eyes—ouch.

IN THE WOODS IS PERPETUAL YOUTH.
—RALPH WALDO EMERSON

- Dust baking soda on other areas to help dry moisture and prevent skin irritation. Baking soda is antibacterial and anti-inflammatory. Absorbent powder (avoid talc-based) is available for the genital area.

- To absorb sweat on your scalp, use dry shampoo. Skip a hat and keep your head cool.

- To keep feet dry, wear breathable shoes with sweat-wicking inserts.

- After your hike, take a shower and finish with the water as cool as you can stand. It will lower your core temperature and help you stop sweating sooner.

- Besides these tips, you should plan to spend two to three weeks acclimating to the heat. Other than that, there is not much you can do about heavy sweating during exercise. Grab your water bottle and get outside. Embrace your sweaty self and be thankful your body is doing its job.

HIKING IN THE RAIN

- When it is rainy, your first thought might not be, "Let's hike!" But with a good attitude, you can learn to love hiking in the rain. As with all other hiking, it is about preparation and planning, including appropriate clothing and gear.

  - Remember that staying dry is easier than getting dried out after you get wet. Be prepared and cautious. If there is lightning, know where to take safe cover (see the "Weather Basics" section).

  - In some areas, like canyons, double-check the forecast for flash flood warnings. Know where you can get to higher ground.

- Start with the Ten Essentials and add what you need to protect your gear: a backpack/daypack rain cover, waterproof case for phone and/or GPS, ziplock plastic bags or dry sacks for other items, and trash bags. The last one is essential on a rainy day, as it can serve a variety of uses. An umbrella may be smart to have, too.

- Have a wicking multi-towel or bandanna for wiping or drying off wet gear.

- Trekking poles are especially helpful when leaves and rocks are wet or you have a creek or other small body of water to cross.

- When you reach a creek crossing, be sure to unbuckle the hip/waist belt of your pack before you start across. If the water has a fast-moving current, you can get free of the pack if you slip.

- Wet feet are more susceptible to blisters, so bring blister supplies and extra socks that you keep dry in your pack. Pack extra clothing, too.

- No cotton in wet weather, no matter the temperature—not even underwear. Wear a wicking material (nylon, polyester, wool).

- Research your outerwear, which should be durable water repellent (DWR). Look for synthetic insulation that is water-resistant for your jacket. If your rainwear needs it, renew its DWR coating. If your jacket cuffs have Velcro or  cinching, seal them when rain comes down hard. Push up the long sleeves of the layer under your jacket to prevent leaking water from crawling up the fabric. Allow some sweat vapor to escape by ventilating a little—loosening the bottom of the jacket and opening the top zipper a bit.

- Consider wearing rain pants. Otherwise, carry an extra pair of dry pants.

  - Even if your outerwear has a brimmed hood, carry a rain hat with a broad brim or a baseball cap in your pack for under the hood.

  - Waterproof footwear and mesh footwear are good choices, with deep lug soles for better traction. You could wear gaiters to protect your socks and the top of your footwear. But, honestly, you have to accept having wet feet to some degree.

- If it will make the hike more enjoyable, switch to dry clothes midway.

- You will need to eat and drink more often than you would in sunny weather. If you don't want to actually stop, drink and snack while you are hiking.

- If you start to feel chilled, add layers and eat a snack. Don't push yourself to finish if a storm makes hiking miserable or hazardous.

- Completely dry out your clothing and gear after hiking in the rain. Mildew and mold grow in hidden places if not dried completely, and that ruins gear.

USING THE REST STEP

- Sometimes a hill is so steep that you cannot climb it without constantly stopping, no matter how slowly you are hiking.

  - Continuous movement is a great strain on your muscles. Stopping and starting, like slowing down and speeding up, wastes energy. The key to preserving your energy is to be a tortoise, not a hare.

  - Employ the rest step, which at first will seem like an awkward start-and-stop motion. But if done correctly, you will be able to hike steeply uphill for a longer distance without stopping.

- Begin the rest step from a stationary upright position.

- Step forward with your right leg, relaxing the muscles in that leg. Keep the weight on the left (back) leg, with the knee almost locked.

- Pause before taking the next step, keeping the weight on your back leg.

- Transfer the weight to your right leg.

- Push yourself up with your right leg and swing your left leg forward to take the next step.

- Keep your right knee almost locked so that the right (now back) leg is bearing all your weight.

- Pause with your weight on your right leg.

- Now transfer the weight to your left leg.

- Push yourself up with your left leg and swing your right leg forward to take the next step.

- Synchronize your breathing with each movement. Inhale deeply as you step up; exhale fully into the rest step.

- Continue climbing this way with a slow, steady pace. The key is to get into a rhythm of doing the same thing for each step. It may take some time to master this.

- Stay in the pause position for however long it takes to avoid running out of breath.

- The almost-locked knee on the rear leg provides support for your weight without requiring help from the leg muscles. That means your leg, hip, and back muscles get a rest—if only for a moment.

- You can get the hang of the rest step by practicing it at home. After a hike (or run or bike ride), when your leg muscles are tired, try the rest step when you are going up steps. Notice how the burn in the quadriceps is substantially reduced.

FUN FACT
Hiking at a normal pace burns approximately 300 calories an hour.

HIKING IN DIFFICULT TERRAIN

- Hiking often involves going around obstacles, but sometimes you must cross difficult terrain such as boulder fields and rock scrambles.

- Good balance, attention to footing, finding a safe route, and confidence are important to hiking in difficult terrain. Use trekking poles to help you keep your balance in these situations.

- Look for the line of least resistance, and use your trekking poles to pick your way through tricky steps and drops.

- Some trails require you to use both your hands and legs to scramble up rocks. You must test hand- and footholds for security before committing your weight. Keep your body, especially your lower body, close to the rock. Push up with your legs. Always maintain three points of contact with the rock.

- Keep your cool when you feel fearful. Take a moment to catch your breath and calm down. Take some time to study your route options. Check that there is a way to turn back.

- Never push your partner(s) to do something that is unsafe or too difficult for them. Respect their limitations and experience level.

- Boulder-hopping may work in some places. It is basically hopping lightly from boulder to boulder using your arms or trekking poles to stay balanced. Look for a route that has a series of evenly sized boulders.

- Scree is a mass of loose, small rocks that is often found above the tree line on mountain slopes. It slides underfoot; for every step up the slope, you may slide two steps back down. You can learn methods for traversing scree: zigzag paths, walking sideways, feet spread-eagled, and kick steps.

- Screeing is a technique where you let gravity do the work, descending in a part-slide, part-slow-motion-jog. Watch some online videos on ascending and descending scree to learn more.

- To avoid getting small rocks in your boots or shoes, wear gaiters that cover the top of your footwear.

- Though most hiking trails avoid bogs, marshland, quicksand, and other waterlogged ground, it is best to know what to do if faced with these conditions. If there is no way around, look for a route through.

- Wet ground is uneven, and the footsteps of previous hikers may tell you how deep and soft the soil might be. Aim for natural hard spots in the soft ground, like rocks, shrubs, trees, and tussocks of hard grass.

- If you start to sink in mud or quicksand, try to run across using rocks, shrubs, trees, and/or grass tussocks to get to safety.

- If you fall into mud or quicksand, remember that it is just saturated ground. Stay afloat with swimming strokes until you find a place to scramble out. Look for logs, rocks, or tussocks of grass to grab onto.

- You may encounter areas of mud and sand exposed at low tide and flooded at high tide. Be careful of crossing when the tide is rising. Check tidal reports in advance so you can avoid crossing an area at one tide level and then finding you are unable to cross back until hours later.

  - Guidebooks and the internet offer local tide tables with the times of the high and low tides. Usually, there is a safe window of 2 to 3 hours in which to cross both ways.

  - Cross tidal flats in bare feet, wet shoes, sports sandals, or mesh footwear, as your feet will get soaked even at low tide.

WILDLIFE SAFETY TIPS

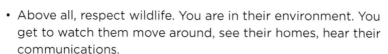

- Remember that most animals are faster than humans. Never feed wildlife. Do not wear strong scents.

- Always take extra precautions if an animal you encounter has babies with it. Stay even farther away. Animals become more territorial and protective with their young.

- Above all, respect wildlife. You are in their environment. You get to watch them move around, see their homes, hear their communications.

- Close encounters with some wildlife can be bothersome or dangerous, and you need information on handling both situations.

- Research the area if you are traveling to a new place. Knowing what wildlife may be there helps you prepare. Take a course about what to do in various wildlife encounters.

- In some areas, the animals to watch for are black bears, grizzly (brown) bears, cougars/mountain lions, wolves, coyotes, bison, moose, elk, mountain goats, snakes, insects—especially mosquitoes and bees—ticks, spiders, and scorpions. (If you are in scorpion country, always shake out your footwear before putting them on.)

- There are others, like deer, mice, raccoons, and skunks, that are less threatening but require your awareness. Stop when you see a deer, skunk, or raccoon. Give the animal a chance to run away. For deer, if you can grab something like a rock and throw it off to the side as a distraction, the animal may move away from you. If a deer approaches, you should leave, as that behavior may indicate something is wrong with the animal. For a skunk, back away very slowly and steadily. Do

not turn your back, make sudden movements, raise your arms, or run. If you must go around it, try to put about 10 feet between you and the

skunk, but do not rush. For a raccoon, if it appears aggressive, back away quickly. Do everything you can to get away from the animal and avoid contact. If the raccoon pursues you, use any outer clothing you may have (like a jacket) to cover your arms, neck, face, and head. Having a sturdy jacket and pepper spray is probably the best way to fend off an attack from a rabid raccoon.

- Many animals will not attack unless they are provoked or feel threatened. Stay a safe distance away. That photo you want to take is not worth the stress you put on the animal or the risk you are taking. The general rule is to stay at least 100 yards away from bears, cougars/mountain lions, and wolves; 25 yards away from all other large animals such as bison, elk, moose, and mountain goats; and 500 feet from squirrels and chipmunks.

- Travel in groups to minimize wildlife encounters. This also adds to the noise factor. Keep children and pets close by. Do not allow them to run ahead and potentially surprise wildlife. Follow leash laws. They are there to protect you and your pets from predators.

- Stay vigilantly aware with all of your senses. Do not wear headphones or earbuds while you are hiking.

- Watch for animal tracks, digs, and droppings that indicate animals are active in the area. Study up in a guidebook or online before you go into an area with potentially dangerous wildlife.

FUN FACT

Ticks will hang on to their host for as long as they can; if one remains for over 24 hours, there is a serious risk of Lyme disease.

- Walk, don't run or jog, in places with potentially dangerous wildlife. Running stimulates a predator's instinct to chase and attack.

- When you are hiking, backpacking, or camping, make sure your food is properly stored. That goes for anything with a scent, too, like toiletries. If you are a camper or backpacker and carry food and cook meals, you'll need special containers and training in protecting the food and yourself from attracting unwanted wildlife.

- Follow Leave No Trace principles. Properly dispose of human waste to avoid attracting wildlife.

- Make noise to avoid surprising a bear or other animal on the trail. If you are in bear territory, walk along saying, "Hey, bear!" every few minutes. You can talk, sing, clap your hands, ring a bell, or strike trekking poles together.

- Avoid hiking at dawn or dusk, when animals and insects are most active. Do not hike after dark in cougar/mountain lion country.

- To keep bugs away, use repellents, netting, long pants and long-sleeved shirts, and clothing treated with repellent, and don't wear scented products.

- Carry bear spray and be sure you have practiced using it before going on the hike.

- After your hike, let a ranger or local agency know if you saw dangerous or unexpected wildlife.

ANIMAL ENCOUNTERS

- As mentioned, the general rule is to stay at least 100 yards away from bears, cougars/mountain lions, and wolves; 25 yards away from all other animals such as bison, elk, moose, and mountain goats; and 500 feet from squirrels and chipmunks. If you've seen large predators in a park, report the sighting(s) to park officials. They will appreciate knowing what you saw.

- Know what animals you might see on your hike and learn how to react to each one. Some encounters require eye contact and others not; for most encounters, the advice is to back away slowly, but if attacked, there are a few instances when running is recommended.

- In a surprise bear encounter, back away slowly, keeping your eyes on the bear or other animal. Bears will generally flee when they sense human presence but, like all animals, can be unpredictable and dangerous. If you see cubs, retreat. If you have bear spray, get it ready.

- With black bears, mountain lions, and other animals that are heading toward you, raise your arms to look taller/larger and make a lot of noise by yelling, throwing objects, or banging pots. Don't make eye contact, though. If you have food and that is what the animal wants, ditch it and move away.

- Grizzly (a subspecies of brown) bears are very large and have a prominent shoulder hump, short ears, a concave face, and long straight claws. Do not yell or make eye contact if you encounter one. Talk quietly and back away slowly. If a brown bear attacks and you don't have bear spray or bear spray fails to deter the bear, play dead.

- Black bears have no shoulder hump and have a straight face profile. If a black bear attacks, do not play dead. Fight back with sticks, rocks, or punches to the bear's eyes and nose.

- Cougars, also known as mountain lions or pumas, are rarely seen and will typically retreat, and attacks are rare. If you do see one, back away, not taking your eyes off it. Absolutely do not run. Pick up small children or move them behind you. Make yourself appear large by raising your arms above your head, or even standing on something to make yourself look taller. Speak calmly and slowly back away. If it moves toward you, shout and throw things.

- If a cougar attacks, fight back. Stay upright if you can and use whatever is available—backpack, rocks, sticks, water bottle, and your hands. If you have bear spray, aim for the cougar's face.

- Bison may be found in the western United States. Stay 25 yards away and wait for them to leave the area, or back away slowly. If they seem upset or attack, find cover behind a boulder or tree (or in a tree), protecting your head and neck.

- Mountain goats live in the western United States, Alaska, and Canada. Like most animals, they shy away from human contact, but some smells attract them, like sweat or urine. Stay away from them, and if approached, slowly back away. If a goat comes toward you, make loud noises, wave clothes, throw rocks, and try to chase it off. Use whatever you can to keep it back and avoid the sharp horns.

- Elk in the northwestern and western United States will attack if threatened, especially during the fall mating season. Keep your distance and back away slowly; do not turn your back. Hide behind a tree or boulder. Always protect your head and neck.

- Moose will defend themselves if they feel threatened. If you see a moose but it does not see you, stay quiet and move away. If the moose sees you, talk to it softly and move away slowly. If a moose charges, it is often bluffing. Hide behind a tree or boulder; if there is nowhere to hide, run. A moose will not chase you far. If it knocks you down, curl up in a ball with your hands and arms wrapped around your head.

- Snakes, like other animals, are usually nonconfrontational. They are often nonvenomous. Rattlesnakes are venomous; if you see one or surprise one (or are unsure what the snake is), stop moving and remain calm. Slowly back away, allowing a safe distance for the snake to leave. Look for an alternate route/detour, going way around where the snake is/was.

- Coyotes typically hunt at night and steer clear of humans, even if hunting in a pack. If you hike at night, make noise so you don't catch a coyote or another potentially dangerous animal unawares. If you see a coyote, raise your arms, backpack, or jacket over your head to make yourself look bigger. Calmly and slowly back away, and maintain eye contact. Do not turn your back and do not run. Unlike bears and cougars, coyotes can be intimidated, and standing your ground, looking large, and maintaining eye contact will likely send the coyote on its way. If it attacks, throw everything you can at it—backpack, rocks, sticks. Fight back and do not play dead.

- Though the big beasts like bears sound scary, the animals most likely to give you trouble are the little creatures: chipmunks, mice, and squirrels. When you take a break, they can scurry into your backpack if they smell food or other scented items. Whatever you do, don't feed or pet any animals in the wild.

- Canada geese are the most aggressive type of wild goose. Geese are very protective of themselves and their young and may hiss and approach humans, pecking and biting. Give geese plenty of space and run away. Do not stand your ground.

- The most common animal encounter you will likely have on a trail is an off-leash dog running or hiking with a human. Dogs are supposed to be on a leash in most parks and trails, and a dog owner who lets a dog off the leash had better have a well-behaved dog that they can control with a voice command. If an off-leash dog comes at you agitated, barking, or moving quickly, say a friendly hello to the dog and owner, even if you are angry at this off-leash occurrence. Stay calm, because dogs sense fear and may become more aggressive. Do not run. Stand tall and still like a tree, standing sideways to the dog if possible (so it is in your peripheral vision), as this is less threatening to an aggressive dog. Lower your hand with a closed fist so the dog may sniff you as it passes. Raise a knee to protect yourself if the dog jumps on you.

MIX IT UP:

- Hike different combinations of the colored trails.

- Hike a short trail one way and then reverse.

- Hike a challenge that your state sets up.

- Hike a theme, such as trails with bridges or boardwalks.

PLANT ENCOUNTERS

- Resist the urge to pick pretty flowers or plants on the trail. Leaving plants as you found them is an essential part of Leave No Trace. But since you are in the wild, it would be nearly impossible not to touch any plant at all, accidentally or otherwise. Avoid unnecessary injury or a painful condition by learning to identify dangerous plants.

- Before you go hiking, learn about the poisonous plants in the area.

- If you know that you may encounter poison ivy and/or poison oak on the hike, wear long-sleeved clothing. If you wear shorts, pull your socks up as high as you can to protect your legs. Poison ivy and oak are the two most dangerous plants you should be aware of. They are poisonous from the roots to the berries.

- A popular identifying phrase for avoiding poison ivy and poison oak is "leaves of three, let it be," referring to those plants having three leaves on a single stem. Poison sumac is red with green leaves and grows as a tall shrub or short tree. Look at images of real plants so you can positively identify what you see out on a hike. One great resource is www.poison-ivy.org; the website describes what is likely to be in your area and has pictures of the plants.

- Poison ivy, oak, and sumac contain urushiol, which can be spread by touching the plant itself or by touching gear that has sap on it, like a backpack or trekking poles.

- Stinging nettle (wood nettle) is also to be avoided. If you brush up against it, it zaps you with poison and feels like a mild bee sting. If a fern is nearby, you can try rubbing the underside of a fern leaf against the stung area.

- Cacti should be avoided, as they have sharp spines and some can cause an itching sensation. If this happens, calamine lotion or baking soda can be used to neutralize the effect.

- Other poisonous plants are manchineel tree, giant hogweed, oleander, castor bean (seeds), holly (berries), poison parsley/hemlock, and water hemlock/cowbane.

- If you've touched a poisonous plant, don't touch your face or eyes. Quickly wash the area with warm water and soap. You want to remove the oils as soon as possible. Itching may be relieved by calamine lotion, apple cider vinegar, or tea tree oil.

- Remove and wash your clothes and hands, especially under the fingernails. Clean all gear that came in contact with the plant.

- Clean your pet, too. Though relatively few animals have a sensitivity to poison ivy, the urushiol will stay on their coat and then rub off on you. If your pet takes a jaunt through any suspect plants, definitely give it a bath when you are done with the hike.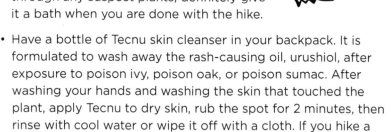

- Have a bottle of Tecnu skin cleanser in your backpack. It is formulated to wash away the rash-causing oil, urushiol, after exposure to poison ivy, poison oak, or poison sumac. After washing your hands and washing the skin that touched the plant, apply Tecnu to dry skin, rub the spot for 2 minutes, then rinse with cool water or wipe it off with a cloth. If you hike a lot, Tecnu is a very wise investment.

- You may think you recognize the berries you see, but refrain from picking them. They belong to the animals that live there. Plus, you may not be sure you ate what you think you ate—and it could be poisonous.

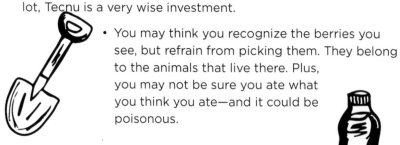

- Same with mushrooms—don't eat or touch them, no matter how hungry you are or how much they look like the ones you get in the grocery store. There are thousands of varieties of mushrooms, and many will send you to the hospital or kill you with just a nibble. Leave them all alone.

- General rule: Do not pick or eat any plant in the wild.

- Hiking at times when flowers, plants, and trees start to or are in bloom means pollen is in the air. Even though you may have immunity to allergic reactions, you should always carry an antihistamine in your first-aid kit. You never know when you might encounter a new species that causes your throat and eyes to swell.

- Be sure to get to a physician or medical facility if you are unsure about a plant encounter and your reaction to it.

MOVING ON TO BACKPACKING

- Backpacking blends hiking with camping. If you are ready to broaden your horizons and want to do more than day hikes, here are the first things you need to know. The main difference from day hikes is the size of your pack and what is in it. It is also important to condition yourself to walk with a fully loaded backpack.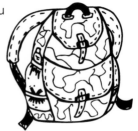

- For beginning backpackers, choose an easy destination close to home that does not include a difficult hike—limit miles and elevation. Choose a well-traveled trail and well-established camp with access to water.

- Some state and national parks have backcountry campsites within a mile or so of a car campground. This is an excellent option for moving into backpacking.

- Go in the most temperate weather possible, ideally midsummer to maximize daylight hours and comfortable conditions. Check, check, and double-check the weather forecasts before the trip.

- If you have an experienced backpacking friend, invite them along. Having a backpacking partner makes the trip safer and more fun, plus builds your knowledge. Starting out, don't bring your furry friend. Keep things simple when you are a beginning backpacker.

- Borrow or rent as much gear as you can starting out. This saves money and lets you gradually work out what you need and want and where you'd like to invest your money. This does not include footwear and your backpack; those need to be your own for fit and comfort.

- Make sure you have the Ten Essentials and brush up on Leave No Trace principles. You will also need a tent, sleeping bag, sleeping pad, stove and fuel, kitchen supplies, and a water treatment method.

- Plan your food carefully. For an overnight trip, you will need a dinner, a breakfast, and a couple of lunches. Don't get too fancy. You can start off with just-add-water meals or freeze-dried backpacking food. Bring plenty of snacks for the trail.

- Practice in the backyard with the stove and fuel you will use.

- You should have containers (or a bear canister) to secure all food and scented products during your trip. Put these items in a stuff sack that you hang from a high tree branch with a nylon cord.

- Get your camping permit (if required). Create or find a backpacking checklist for primary gear, navigation and emergency gear, clothing, food and water, sun/bug protection, bathroom supplies, tools and repair supplies, and other essentials. After your trip, make notes on the checklist of what worked and what didn't. Soon you'll have a personalized checklist for future trips.

- Pack clothing to wear in camp. This can be one of your layers or extra clothes you pack, plus camp shoes like water sandals or ultralight sneakers.

- Do plenty of day hikes prior to your first backpack adventure. You need to be able to handle trails of a similar distance and elevation gain to your planned trip, wearing a backpack loaded with 30-plus pounds. There are strength exercises you can do to prepare for backpacking, too.

- The loaded backpack should not be more than 20 percent of your body weight. Learn how to pack and hoist a backpack properly and practice both a number of times before the trip.

- Be mentally ready. The more preparation and planning you put in, the more you will be in the right mindset. Practice with all your gear—pitching the tent, using the stove, filtering water.

- You need to learn basic first aid and map and compass navigation, and have emergency situation knowledge.

- Pack early and use that checklist. Confirm that all your devices have fresh batteries and are charged. Make sure you have the additional gear and extra clothing, food, and water to keep you safe and happy.

- Leave your itinerary with a family member or friend. Include the details of where you are going, where you will park, and when you expect to be back. Plan a post-trip check-in.

CELEBRATE HIKING:

- Combine a hike with a picnic or outdoor eatery.

- Celebrate by joining a First Day event (New Year's Day).

- Celebrate by participating on Trails Day (first Saturday in June).

- Thank organizations that maintain your trails.

GLOSSARY OF TERMS

access: a trail that connects a main trail to a town, road, or another trail or trail system

acclimate: to gradually become more comfortable in different physical conditions or weather

altimeter: an instrument for determining the altitude attained

altitude: the height of a point in relation to sea level or ground level; the vertical or up distance

backcountry: wilderness and sparsely inhabited rural areas; also describes primitive, undeveloped trails and campsites

backpacking: the outdoor recreation of carrying gear on one's back while hiking for more than a day

base layer: the layer of clothing closest to the skin, providing a layer of warmth while keeping skin dry

base weight: the total weight of all the gear, food, water, etc., put in a backpack

bearing: the horizontal direction of one point with respect to another or to a compass; also, a determination of one's position

bivy (aka bivouac, bivvy): a temporary shelter or improvised campsite; also refers to a bivouac sack, a tarp-like shelter carried by hikers for use as emergency shelter

bivy bag (aka bivy sack): a collapsible bag made of weatherproof fabric that is used to provide shelter, usually for a single person, in the wilderness

bladder: a hydration pack's reservoir, typically made of rubber or plastic

blaze (aka marker, marking): a mark used to identify a trail, such as a spot of paint on a tree or rock

book time: an estimate of the time required to hike a trail

breathability: a fabric's ability to allow air to pass through

bushwhack: to hike off-trail, especially through underbrush that may have to be cut to traverse

cache: a waterproof container containing items for geocaching

cairn: a pile of stones used to mark a trail, especially in an area where there is often fog or snow, making blazes less easy to see

cat hole (cathole): a pit dug with a trowel or stick for human feces, away from water sources and camp, and covered

compass: an instrument used for navigation and orientation that shows direction relative to the geographic cardinal directions (points)

compression straps: on a backpack, webbing straps that crisscross the sides of the pack and are used to compress the load closer to the pack frame, bringing the weight and bulk nearer to one's back for better balance, comfort, and weight transfer when walking

contour line: a line on a map joining points of equal height (elevation) above or below sea level

CPR (cardiopulmonary resuscitation): a medical procedure involving repeated compression of a patient's chest, performed in an attempt to restore blood circulation and breathing; an emergency procedure of external cardiac massage and artificial respiration for someone who has no pulse and has stopped breathing

crampon: a set of metal spikes to put on footwear for traction assistance in climbing on snow and ice

day hike: a hike that can be completed in a single day or less

declination (magnetic declination): the angle on the horizontal plane between magnetic north and true north, which varies depending on one's position on the Earth's surface and changes over time

dehydration: a deficit of total body water when water loss exceeds water intake, which also disrupts metabolic processes

denier: a unit of measure for the linear mass density of fibers; for some fabrics indicates opaqueness from ultra sheer to thick opaque

DEET (diethyltoluamide): a common active ingredient in insect repellents, applied to the skin or clothing as protection against biting insects such as chiggers, fleas, leeches, mosquitoes, and ticks

difficulty level: the rating of a hiking trail's suitability for hikers with varying fitness and experience; there are different combinations of ratings, such as easy, moderate, challenging, difficult, very difficult, extreme

directional arrow: a sign showing an arrow pointing the direction to follow

down fill power: a unit of measure for the loft or relative quality of a down product, specifically its insulating efficiency; the higher the fill power, the more air a certain weight of the down can trap

DWR (durable water repellent): a type of fabric coating that adds water resistance, commonly used with waterproof breathable fabrics such as Gore-Tex to prevent the outer layer from becoming saturated

elevation: the height of an area of land, especially above sea level

elevation gain (aka cumulative gain): the sum of the gain in elevation for an entire hiking trip

exposure: the state of being in a situation in which something harmful or dangerous might affect you

filter: a device that physically strains protozoan cysts and bacteria from water

firestarter: material for starting a fire, which ranges from waterproof matches, butane lighter, cotton balls, and a chemical like alcohol to metal or wood used to ignite a fire

first aid: emergency care or treatment given to an injured or ill person before professional medical help can be obtained

gaiters: a fabric leg covering that goes from the instep to above the ankle, calf, or knee as protection from precipitation, insects, or animals

geocaching: a competitive sport in which participants are given geographical coordinates of a cache of items that they search for with a GPS device

Gore-Tex: a trademark of W. L. Gore & Associates for a synthetic waterproof fabric permeable to air and water vapor, used in outdoor clothing

gorp: a snack of high-energy food, such as raisins, nuts, or a combination trail mix

GPS (Global Positioning System): a navigation system using satellite signals to fix the location of a radio receiver on (or above) the Earth's surface

greenway (aka urban trail): a trail established along a natural corridor, such as a river, stream, ridgeline, canal, rail trail, or conservation route, which can connect with residential or business areas

heading: the course or direction in which a moving object is pointed, usually expressed as a compass reading in degrees

headlamp: a light source affixed to one's head with a band, for seeing in nighttime or dark conditions while hiking, powered by batteries or rechargeable

high point: the point of the highest elevation in a given area or on a given hiking trip

hot spot: a painful, red skin irritation caused by excessive friction that can develop into a blister

hydration: the process of taking in or supplying water

hydration pack: a system for water intake, built in or added to a backpack, composed of a flexible bladder (reservoir) and a hose or valve for drinking water from the bladder

itinerary: a plan for a trip that one is going to take, including about when and where one will travel, where one will park, and when one expects to return

junction: a point where two or more trails join

layer: a set of clothing (upper and lower, usually) for outdoor activities; e.g., base layer (underwear), middle layer (insulation), and outer layer (protection)

Leave No Trace: a set of outdoor principles promoting conservation in the outdoors

loop: a hiking route that allows a user to end up where they started with either minimal or no repetition of the trails

magnetic north: the direction in which the north end of a compass needle will point in response to the Earth's magnetic field; this point deviates from true north over time and in different places because the Earth's magnetic poles are not fixed in relation to its axis

moisture-wicking: describing the ability of some fabrics to pull moisture away from the skin using tiny, built-in capillaries

navigation: a way to find and follow a trail or path through a place; the skill of using a map and compass, GPS, or nature's signs to find and go in a particular direction

orienteering: a competitive sport in which participants find their way to various checkpoints in the wilderness in the lowest elapsed time with the aid of a map and compass

out-and-back (aka in-and-out): a hiking trail that goes from point A (trailhead) to point B and then back to point A along the same trail

paracord (aka parachute cord, 550 cord): a lightweight nylon rope originally used in the suspension lines of parachutes that is now used as a general purpose utility cord

permethrin: a pesticide/insecticide sprayed on clothing and gear to kill ticks and mosquitoes that touch the fabric

point-to-point (aka destination trail): a hiking route designed to be walked from one place to another and considered too long to return to the starting point

potable water: drinking water; any water that is safe to drink or use for food preparation; tap water

privy (aka outhouse): an outdoor toilet

ramble: another word for hike or a pleasure walk

ripstop nylon: a synthetic fabric woven in a cross-hatched pattern to prevent small rips and holes from expanding

scale: the ratio of a distance on a map to the corresponding distance on the ground

scree: small loose stones in a mass on a slope of a mountain; a slope covered with small loose stones

section hiking: a method of hiking a long-distance trail (a thru-hike) in stages or segments, either due to time, ease, or pace factors, or to avoid crowds and certain weather and seasonal conditions

shakedown: a shorter trip taken by a prospective thru-hiker or backpacker to test gear/equipment for trail worthiness

shoulder season: a travel period between peak and off-peak seasons, depending on the area but considered to be sometime in March to late May and from mid-September to late November

spur trail (aka side trail): a trail that branches off the main trail and has a dead end; that is, it does not loop or connect to another trail; often leads to points of interest such as overlooks or campsites

stacked-loop trail: a series of several, interconnected loop trails offering users the option of not traveling the same section of trail more than once on a trip

summit: the highest point of a hill or mountain

switchback: a trail up a steep hill or mountain that is in a zigzag pattern instead of straight so that it reduces the slope (overall gradient) of the steep terrain and makes it easier to climb

synthetic fiber: any fiber made by humans through chemical processes, as opposed to natural fibers derived from living organisms

talus: a sloping mass of rock fragments at the foot of a cliff

terrain: the geographic landscape and its physical features

thru-hike: a long-distance trail completed in one or more seasons

topographic map: a type of map characterized by large-scale detail and quantitative representation of relief, usually using contour lines and other methods

torso length: a body measurement used to size and fit backpacks—the distance in inches between a person's C7 vertebra at the back of the neck and the top of the hipbone

trail (aka path, track): an unpaved footpath, lane, or road used for walking and hiking

trailhead: the spot where a trail begins

tread: the actual walking surface of the trail; the native material of soil, grass, organic matter, and/or stone that is constructed or smoothed to a trail standard

tree line (aka timberline): the upper limit of tree growth in high elevations and high latitudes; the edge of the habitat at which trees are capable of growing

trek: a journey made on foot, especially a difficult one

trekking pole (aka hiking pole/hiking stick/walking pole): a piece of hiking gear used singly or in a pair to assist the hiker with walking rhythm, balance, and stability on variable and rough terrain

ultralight: denoting any hiking gear (backpack, trekking poles, tent, etc.) that is extremely lightweight

water treatment: any process used to improve the quality of water to make it acceptable and safe for drinking and cooking

waterproof-breathable fabric: a fabric consisting of an inner layer that faces the wearer, a middle layer of nylon or polyester, and an outer layer that protects the laminate; the clothing resists liquid water passing through but allows water vapor to evaporate

waypoint: any stopping place or intermediate point on a route or trail; a specific location's (trailhead, junction, summit, campsite) coordinates used to navigate during a trip

BIBLIOGRAPHY AND RESOURCES

Backpacker Magazine Day Hiker's Handbook, Michael Lanza, Mountaineers Books, 2003

Complete Idiot's Guide to Backpacking and Hiking, Jason Stevenson, Alpha, 2010

The Complete Walker IV, Colin Fletcher, Knopf, 2002

Eyewitness Backpacking and Hiking, Karen Berger, DK, 2005

On the Trail: A History of American Hiking, Silas Chamberlin, Yale, 2019

The Hiking Companion, Michael W. Robins, Storey, 2003

The Honest Backpacker, James Klopovic, self-published, Affinitas LLC, 2017

Trailside Guide: Hiking & Backpacking, Karen Berger, W. W. Norton, 2003

ABOUT THE AUTHOR

Barbara Ann Kipfer is an archaeologist, lexicographer, hiker, author, and former sportswriter. She has written more than sixty-five books and calendars, mostly lists, including *14,000 Things to Be Happy About, 5,203 Things to Do Instead of Looking at Your Phone, Self-Meditation, Instant Karma, 8,789 Words of Wisdom, The Wish List, 4,000 Questions for Getting to Know Anyone and Everyone, Roget's International Thesaurus*, and *1,001 Ways to Live Wild, 1,001 Ways to Slow Down*, and *1,001 Ways to Be Creative*. Find more of Barbara's work online at thingstobehappyabout.com.